CW00505961

MOCKTAIL RECIPE BOOK

A Unique Collection of 205 Tasty Non-Alcoholic Drinks
Recipes for Kids, Adults & Whole Family

Avril D. Muro

Table of Content

INTRODUCTION

A mocktail is a non-alcoholic mixed drink. The term "mocktail" is a portmanteau of the words "mock" and "cocktail". A mocktail can be made with various juices, syrups, and soda.

Mocktails became popular in the United States during the Prohibition era when the sale of alcohol was illegal. Mocktails were created as an alternative to alcoholic drinks.

Today, mocktails are popular among non-alcoholic drinkers as well as those searching for a non-alcoholic alternative to cocktails. Mocktails are suitable for persons of all ages.

This mocktail recipe book is a unique collection of 205 tasty non-alcoholic drinks recipes for kids, adults, and the whole family. Recipes in this book are easy to prepare and follow.

Some of the recipes in this book include:

- Cranberry Mocktail

- Pineapple Mocktail

- Orange Mocktail

- Lemon Mocktail

- Strawberry Mocktail

- Grapefruit Mocktail

With this recipe book, you can make delicious mocktails that everyone will enjoy. So, this book is for you whether you are looking for a non-alcoholic alternative to cocktails or simply want to produce something unique for the children.

1. APPLE CIDER MARGARITA

Total Time 10 Mins

Servings 3

INGREDIENTS

For the margarita

- 3 whole limes juiced
- 4 cups of apple cider; ensure there is no additional sugar!

For the fancy rim

- ⅓ cup of coconut sugar
- 2 tbsp cinnamon

INSTRUCTIONS

For the fancy rim:

➢ Grab a small bowl and fill it with water first. Then, combine the coconut sugar and cinnamon in another small bowl that is large enough to accommodate dipping the glass. Now, submerge the glass in the water to a depth of approximately 1/4 inch, and then dip it in the combination of cinnamon and coconut sugar.

For the drink:

➢ Mix the lime and apple cider in a bowl, then gently pour the mixture into the cocktail glass with a rim that has been adorned.
➢ Put an ice cube in the drink!
➢ ENJOY!

2. VIRGIN MARGARITA

Total Time: 5 Mins

Servings: 1

INGREDIENTS

- Kosher salt for rimming glass
- 4 ounces simple syrup
- 2 ounces of lime juice
- 1-ounce lemon juice
- 1 ounce of orange juice
- Lime wheels or wedges for garnish

INSTRUCTIONS

➢ Add a tsp of kosher salt on a small plate. Rub a lime wedge over the rim of the glass to moisten it. Coat the rim of the glass evenly with salt.
➢ Pour simple syrup, lime juice, lemon juice, and orange juice into an ice-filled cocktail shaker approximately halfway full.
➢ Cover and vigorously shake for 15 seconds.
➢ Pour into a glass with a rim. Serve with a slice of lime or a lime wheel as a garnish.

NOTES

1. To make by the pitcher, multiply the number of servings you want by the number of liquid ingredients. Stir everything together in a pitcher. Pour into glasses rimmed with salt and filled with ice.

3. SHIRLEY TEMPLE DRINK

Total Time: 5 Mins

Servings: 1

INGREDIENTS

- 1 ounce of grenadine
- small ice cubes
- 4 ounces chilled lemon-lime soda
- 4 ounces chilled ginger ale
- maraschino cherries, for garnish

INSTRUCTIONS

- ➢ Pour the Grenadine into a glass with ice.
- ➢ Add the ginger ale and lemon-lime soda over top.
- ➢ Stir gently to mix.
- ➢ Enjoy with a maraschino cherry on top!

4. TROPICAL PUNCH MOCKTAIL

Total Time: 5 Mins

Serving: 4

INGREDIENTS

- ½ cup of pineapple juice
- 1 thinly sliced orange
- 4 lemongrass stems, bruised
- 4 x 375ml cans chilled Lightly Sparkling Passionfruit
- Mint sprigs, to serve

INSTRUCTIONS

➢ Two 12-hole, 2-tsp ice cube trays were filled with 2 tsp (10 ml) of pineapple juice each. Allow to freeze overnight or until frozen.

➢ In serving glasses, divide the orange slices, pineapple ice cubes, and lemongrass. Pour passionfruit over it. Passionfruit with a little sparkle. To serve, garnish with mint.

5. BLUEBERRY GINGER COOLER

Prep Time: 3 Hrs

Cook Time: 20 Mins

Total Time: 3 Hrs 20 Mins

INGREDIENTS

- 1 liter of water
- 1.25 cups of fresh blueberries
- 1 heaping tbsp of grated ginger
- 4-5 tbsp of sugar, or as desired
- **To serve**
- 2-3 cans of unsweetened lemon-lime sparkling water
- ice cubes
- Mint leaves

INSTRUCTIONS

➢ Over medium-high heat, add water, blueberries, and grated ginger to the skillet. Allow everything to come to a boil.

➢ When the mixture begins to boil, add the sugar and stir until it dissolves.

➢ Reduce the heat to low and mash the blueberries with the back of your spatula. Allow the mixture to boil for another 10-15 minutes after mashing it all together.

➢ Remove the syrup from the heat and set it aside to cool for 2-3 hours, covered with a cling sheet. It is important to do this so that the flavors mix well.

➢ After 2-3 hours, pour the syrup into a transparent bowl. You may now cover it and store it in the refrigerator until ready to use.

➢ Fill ⅔ of the glass with the syrup and ice cubes to serve the blueberry ginger cooler.

- ➢ Then pour in the lemon-lime sparkling water and mix well to incorporate the soda and syrup.
- ➢ Enjoy with fresh blueberries and mint leaves as a garnish!

6. HONEY BLACKBERRY MINT MOCKTAILS

Total Time: 10 Mins

Servings: 4

INGREDIENTS

- 8 fresh blackberries plus more for garnish
- ¼ cup of honey
- A handful of fresh mint leaves, plus more for garnish
- juice of 1 lemon
- ½ cup of water
- 2 cups of seltzer

INSTRUCTIONS

- ➢ Muddle the blackberries, honey, and mint in a cocktail shaker until well combined.
- ➢ Cover and shake to combine the lemon juice and water.
- ➢ Into two glasses with ice, strain the mixture.
- ➢ 1 cup of seltzer is poured into each glass.
- ➢ Serve with blackberries and mint leaves as garnish.

NOTES

1. If you don't have a cocktail shaker or muddler, don't worry. It's no issue! Simply stir the ingredients with a wooden spoon in a small bowl, and then strain the mixture through a mesh sieve.

7. NON-ALCOHOLIC SANGRIA

Total Time: 10 Mins

Servings: 6-8

INGREDIENTS

- Fresh lemon slices
- Fresh lime slices
- Fresh orange slices
- Cranberries
- 2 cups of cranberry juice
- 2 cups of grape juice
- 1 cup of orange juice
- ½ cup of lemon juice
- 4 cups of sparkling mineral water OR lemon-lime soda

INSTRUCTIONS

- ➢ Combine the lemon, lime, orange, and cranberries in a big pitcher. Combine the cranberry juice, grape juice, orange juice, and lemon juice in a bowl. Mix thoroughly.
- ➢ Keep it refrigerated until you're ready to use it.
- ➢ Add the sparkling mineral water or lemon-lime soda just before serving. Combine thoroughly.

NOTES

1. Use soda for a sweeter drink. Use sparkling mineral water if you want a less sweet drink.

8. KIWI MOJITO MOCKTAIL

Total Time: 10 Mins

Servings: 2 - 3

INGREDIENTS

- 2 nos chopped Kiwi
- 1 big lemon
- few spring mint leaves
- 2-3 tbsp of honey
- 300ml of soda water
- Ice cubes as required

INSTRUCTIONS

➤ Slice the lemon in half and slice it thinly. Add one sliced kiwi, half a lemon slice, and a few mints spring or leaves to a mortar and pestle or a cocktail tumbler, then smash or muddle the ingredients together to release the flavors.
➤ Combine the crushed ingredients in a jug or glass with honey, soda water, and ice cubes.
➤ Serve with extra kiwi slices, lemon slices, and mint sprigs on top.

NOTE

1. Add a touch of pepper powder for taste variation.
2. You may crush a piece of ginger or use gingerale instead of soda water.

9. CINDERELLA: A FRUITY MOCKTAIL EVERYONE WILL LOVE

Total Time: 3 Mins

Serving: 1

INGREDIENTS

- 2 tbsp of freshly squeezed lemon juice
- 2 tbsp of freshly squeezed orange juice
- 2 tbsp of pineapple juice
- ½ tbsp grenadine
- ¼ cup of ginger ale, or club soda
- Pineapple and orange slices for garnish

INSTRUCTIONS

- ➢ Collect all of the ingredients.
- ➢ Pour the juices and grenadine into an ice-filled cocktail shaker.
- ➢ Shake vigorously.
- ➢ Fill a cold Collins glass with fresh ice and strain into it.
- ➢ Add the ginger ale on top.
- ➢ Serve with pineapple and/or orange slices as garnish. Enjoy!

NOTE

1. Bartenders and party hosts might want to offer Cinderella to guests who don't drink alcohol or who are driving. It's much more interesting than a Coke or a cup of coffee, and almost everyone will like the way it tastes.

10. STRAWBERRY DAIQUIRIS

Prep Time: 10 Mins

Cook Time: 10 Mins

Additional Time: 30 Mins

Total Time: 50 Mins

Serving: 4

INGREDIENTS

Simple Syrup

- 1 cup of granulated sugar
- 1 cup of water

Daiquiris

- 4 cups of frozen strawberries
- 1 cup of fresh strawberries, washed and hulled
- ½ to ¾ cup of fresh lime juice to taste
- 1 cup of 7up or Sprite

INSTRUCTIONS

Simple Syrup

➤ In a small saucepan, combine the sugar and water and cook, stirring regularly, until the sugar has dissolved, about 5 minutes. Take the pan from the heat and set it aside to cool thoroughly. Placing the saucepan in a bigger bowl partially filled with ice, may be done rapidly. The simple syrup may be prepared ahead of time and kept in the refrigerator for at least a few weeks.

Make the daiquiris

➤ In a powerful blender, mix strawberries, lime juice, and soda. To begin, pour in 3/4 cup of simple syrup. Blend until smooth and creamy. To make sure everything gets blended all the way, pause and scrape down the sides or crush the frozen strawberries down into the blender blades at the bottom several times.

➤ Taste and adjust the sweetness with extra simple syrup (if desired) or lime juice (if you want it tarter). For serving, pour into glasses and top with a slice of lime and a strawberry.

11. STRAWBERRY ORANGE GINGER FIZZ

Prep Time: 10 Mins

Cook Time: 10 Mins

Total Time: 20 Mins

Serving: 4

INGREDIENTS

For the syrup

- 8 ounces of hulled and quartered strawberries
- 3 inches of peeled and sliced fresh ginger
- Three 3-inch orange peel strips, peeled with a vegetable peeler
- ⅓ cup of honey
- ¼ cup of fresh-squeezed orange juice
- ¼ cup of water
- A pinch of sea salt

For each drink

- 2-3 tbsp of strawberry, orange, ginger syrup
- 6 ounces of sparkling water
- 2 ice cubes
- Half an orange slice, half a hulled strawberry, and a sprig of mint for serving

INSTRUCTIONS

➢ To prepare the syrup, mix all of the ingredients in a small saucepan over medium heat. Bring to a boil, then reduce to low heat and cook for approximately five minutes, or until the liquid around the strawberries is bright pinkish-red and the strawberries themselves have faded.

➢ Allow the syrup to cool for five minutes before straining it into a bowl or jar using a fine-mesh strainer, pushing on the particles in the sieve with a spoon to remove as much liquid as possible.

➢ Let the syrup to cool to room temperature before consuming, or refrigerate it for up to one week in an airtight container.

> Put 2-3 tsp of syrup into the bottom of an 8-to 10-ounce glass to prepare each drink. If you like, you may start with two tsp and add more later. Pour bubbly water into the glass until it's almost full. Add two ice cubes to the mix. Serve immediately with a split orange slice, half a strawberry, and a sprig of mint as garnish.

12. REFRESHING HIBISCUS MOCKTAIL

Prep Time: 5 Mins

Cook Time: 5 Mins

Total Time: 10 Mins

Serving: 4

INGREDIENTS

- 3 bags of hibiscus tea
- 24 ounces of water
- 4 tbsp of lime juice, plus lime rounds for garnish
- Topo Chico or other sparkling water or club soda
- Ice, for serving

Honey Simple Syrup
- 2 tbsp of honey
- 2 tbsp of water

INSTRUCTIONS

> Heat the water to a low simmer in a teapot or a pan on the stovetop to make the tea component. Discard the tea bags after 3 minutes of steeping in boiling water (or strain off the loose tea). Allow 20 minutes for the tea to cool to room temperature.
> **To make the honey syrup:** In a microwave-safe bowl or small saucepan, mix equal parts honey and water (say, 2 tsp each if you're only preparing one batch of beverages). Warm in the microwave or stovetop until the honey is fully dissolved in the water. Place aside.

➤ Fill four medium glasses with ice when ready to serve. Half-fill each with hibiscus tea. Add 1 tbsp of lime juice and 1 tsp of honey simple syrup to each glass and mix to incorporate. Pour the remaining sparkling water into each glass, gently stirring to mix. Depending on your taste, you may want to add less lime juice or more simple syrup. Serve right away.

NOTES

1. Prepare the tea and honey simple syrup ahead of time and chill them separate until ready to serve. Since sparkling water loses its carbonation over time, I'd recommend mixing the drinks immediately before serving.

13. VIRGIN COSMOPOLITAN MOCKTAIL

Total Time: 5 Mins

Servings: 1

INGREDIENTS

- 90ml Reduced Sugar Cranberry Juice
- 30ml of freshly squeezed lime juice
- 60ml sparkling water
- 30ml of orange juice

INSTRUCTIONS

➤ In a cocktail shaker (a mason jar works excellent!), combine the cranberry juice, lime, and soda. Shake gently with lots of ice.
➤ Pour the mixture into a martini glass.
➤ Serve with a splash of orange juice.

NOTES

1. Use cranberry juice with less sugar to make it healthier.
2. Shake carefully, just enough to incorporate the ingredients. If you shake the cocktail shaker too hard, the carbonation in the soda water can cause the lid to fly off!

14. MARGARITA MOCKTAIL RECIPE

Prep Time: 5 Mins

Cook Time: 5 Mins

Total Time: 10 Mins

Servings: 4

INGREDIENTS

- 2 cups of limeade
- ¾ cup of orange juice
- ¼ cup of simple syrup
- ½ – 1 cup of club soda
- Sugar and coarse salt for the rim
- Lime for garnish
- Ice

INSTRUCTIONS

- Combine limeade, orange juice, and simple syrup in a small pitcher.
- Pour an equal amount of sugar and coarse salt onto a plate.
- Slice the lime and run it over the rim of each glass before dipping it into the sugar/salt combination to coat the rim.
- Fill the glass halfway with ice.
- Fill each glass close to the top with the limeade mixture.
- Finish with a splash of club soda in each glass.
- Squeeze a lime wedge into each drink.

NOTES

1. I used a coarse salt and sugar combination to rim the glasses, and it turned out beautifully!

15. NON-ALCOHOLIC MIMOSA

Total Time: 5 Mins

Servings: 1

INGREDIENTS

- 2 ounces of orange juice
- 2 ounces of pineapple juice
- 4 ounces Orange Flavor Slim Can

INSTRUCTIONS

➢ In a champagne glass, mix all of the ingredients and garnish with an orange slice.

16. VIRGIN PIÑA COLADA RECIPE

Prep Time: 5 Mins

Cook Time: 5 Mins

Total Time: 55 Mins

Servings: 4

INGREDIENTS

- 1 cup of cream of coconut
- ¾ cup of pineapple juice
- 2 tbsp of fresh lime juice
- 1 tsp vanilla extract
- 1 tsp molasses (optional)
- 10 ounces of chopped frozen pineapple
- Maraschino cherries, to garnish (optional)
- fresh chopped pineapple to garnish (optional)

INSTRUCTIONS

➢ Important: If you're making homemade coconut cream, make it first and let it cool before starting with the recipe. See note.

- 1 cup of coconut cream, ¾ cup of pineapple juice, 2 tbsp lime juice, 1 tsp vanilla extract, 1 tsp molasses (optional), and 10 ounces of frozen sliced pineapple (about 3 cups), combined in a blender.
- Mix for one minute or until completely smooth.
- Place the mixture in a jar with a lid. Chill for 45 minutes to an hour or until the mixture is partially frozen.
- Return the mixture to the blender and blend for a few seconds more until the mixture is thick and creamy.
- Serve right away. Maraschino cherries, parasol picks (the official name for the cute umbrellas), straws, and a pineapple wedge serve as garnish.

NOTES

Cream of Coconut Recipe

- 1 can of regular coconut milk (13 ounces) (not lite)
- 1 cup of granulated sugar
- ⅛ tsp kosher salt
1. Note: This cream of coconut recipe makes approximately 2 cups of coconut cream, which you may split evenly between 2 batches. (Because most blenders can't handle that much liquid.)
2. Combine the coconut milk can, 1 cup of sugar, and ⅛ tsp kosher salt in a small pot. Heat for about 5 minutes over medium-low heat or until the sugar is completely dissolved. As the mixture cools, it will thicken.
3. Chill the mixture fully before mixing half of it to make pina Coladas. I prefer to put it in the freezer for an hour or two. Before adding to the blender, stir everything together. If you're only preparing one batch of Pina Coladas, keep the remaining cream of coconut in the refrigerator for up to 5 days or freeze for up to 3 months. Use it the next time you get the craving! If you freeze it, you may need to defrost it slightly before mixing, but you will not need to thaw it completely.
4. Cream of Coconut bought in a store.
5. You can buy pre-made cream of coconut if you don't want to make it. Look for drink mixers in the liquor section of the shop. The most popular brand is Coco Lopez, but Coco Real and Goya also sell it. Use 1 cup or 8 ounces of store-bought coconut cream for one batch of virgin Pina Coladas.

17. FROZEN PEACH BELLINI MOCKTAIL

Total Time: 5 Mins

Servings: 2

INGREDIENTS

- 2 peeled and sliced ripe peaches, (or you can use frozen)
- 1 cup of sparkling apple juice, plus more for serving
- 2 tsp Sugar Blend
- 1 tsp lime juice

INSTRUCTIONS

- Freeze the sliced peaches for 1 hour.
- In a blender, blend peaches, 1 cup of sparkling apple juice, Sugar Blend, and lime juice until smooth.
- Pour into two glasses and top with another ½ inch of sparkling apple juice.

NOTES

1. You may want to use more or less Sugar Blend depending on the sweetness of your peaches and your personal preference. Start with 1 tsp and increase as needed.

18. SUMMER CUP OF MOCKTAIL

Total Time: 15 Mins

Servings: 1

INGREDIENTS

- 1cm thick slice of cucumber
- 1 sprig mint
- few frozen red berries
- 120ml clear, sparkling lemonade
- Ice

To garnish (optional)

- more frozen berries
- chopped fruits
- cucumber slice
- mint
- citrus

INSTRUCTIONS

➢ Finely chop the cucumber and mint sprig. In a small saucepan, bring 200ml water to a boil, then add the mint and cucumber. Remove from the heat and set aside for 2 minutes. Add a small handful of frozen berries, let them to defrost for one minute, and then lightly smash them with the back of a spoon. Take the mixture and strain it. This will keep for up to 24 hours in the fridge and will make four drinks.

➢ In a large glass, pour 40ml of your strained mixture. Top with 120ml lemonade and a handful of ice. Garnish with whatever sliced fruit you choose, as well as more frozen berries and mint leaves, if you have them. To combine, carefully stir everything together.

19. MAI TAI MOCKTAIL PARTY PUNCH RECIPE

Total Time: 5 Mins

Servings: 3

INGREDIENTS

- 1-liter orange juice
- 1-liter pineapple juice
- ½ cup of lime juice
- ½ cup of almond syrup
- ½ cup of grenadine
- 1-liter sparkling/seltzer water
- ice
- oranges, limes, and cherries for garnish

INSTRUCTIONS

➢ In a pitcher, mix orange juice, pineapple juice, lime juice, and almond syrup.

- ➤ This base for punch can be kept in the fridge until it's time to party.
- ➤ When ready to serve, fill a cup halfway with juice, a splash of grenadine, seltzer water, and garnish with fruit.
- ➤ To serve, combine the grenadine and seltzer water with the juice in a large punch bowl and mix well, then add the ice and fruit.

20. REFRESHING ORANGE MINT MOCKTAIL

Total Time: 15 Mins

Servings: 4

INGREDIENTS

- 2 cups of orange juice
- ¼ cup of squeezed lemon juice
- ½ cup of club soda / carbonated water
- ¼ cup of water
- 2 tbsp sugar
- 2-3 slices orange
- 2-3 leaves mint
- ice cubes (as required)

INSTRUCTIONS

- ➤ Mix the orange juice, lemon juice, water, and sugar in a pitcher until the sugar dissolves.
- ➤ Serve with orange slices, mint leaves, and ice cubes.
- ➤ Top with soda.

NOTES

1. This mocktail tastes better if made in advance so that the orange and mint extracts can combine thoroughly.
2. To make the drink fizzy, add soda just prior to serving.
3. Orange juice with pulp is better.

21. SIDECAR MOCKTAIL

Total Time: 5 Mins

Servings: 1

INGREDIENTS

- 50ml of cold Lapsang Souchong tea
- 50ml of lemon juice
- 1 tsp marmalade
- ½ – 1 tsp honey
- ice
- slice dried orange (optional)

INSTRUCTIONS

➤ Chill a coupe glass in the refrigerator. In a cocktail shaker, combine the cold tea, lemon juice, and marmalade; mix to break down the marmalade and allow it to dissolve. Mix the honey in, and then add the ice.

➤ Shake vigorously until the exterior of the shaker feels cold, then double strain into the cooled glass. Serve plain or with a slice of dried orange on top, if desired.

22. FROZEN STRAWBERRY MARGARITAS

Total Time: 5 Mins

Servings: 4

INGREDIENTS

- ⅓ cup of coarse sugar
- 2 cups of hulled and chopped fresh strawberries
- ⅓ cup of fresh orange juice
- 2 tbsp of fresh lime juice
- 2 tbsp of agave
- 1 ½ cups of crushed ice
- 4 fresh strawberries for garnish

INSTRUCTIONS

- ➢ Make the margarita glasses. In a shallow bowl, pour coarse sugar. To coat the rims of the glasses, wet them with a lime slice and press the glass top into the sugar.
- ➢ In a blender, combine the sliced strawberries, orange juice, lime juice, and agave. Pulse several times to combine. Taste and, if needed, add more agave. Pulse in the crushed ice until the required consistency is achieved. Fill the prepared cups with the drink.
- ➢ Decorate each drink with a fresh strawberry with the green leaves on top, cut in half lengthwise from the bottom and put on the lip of each glass before serving.

23. VERY BERRY MOCKTAIL

Total Time: 5 Mins

Servings: 8

INGREDIENTS

- 2 quarts cranberry juice
- 12-ounce thawed pink lemonade concentrate
- 12-ounce sparkling water in Berry
- Crushed or pebbled ice
- Lime wedges (optional)

INSTRUCTIONS

- ➢ In a large serving bowl or pitcher, combine the cranberry juice, pink lemonade, and sparkling water. Garnish with a lime wedge and serve over crushed or pebbled ice.

24. NEW YORK SOUR MOCKTAIL

Total Time: 10 Mins

Servings: 1

INGREDIENTS

- 1 tsp tea leaves
- a few drops of vanilla extract
- 25ml of lemon juice
- 3 tsp maple syrup
- 1 tbsp egg white
- ice
- 10ml of pomegranate juice

INSTRUCTIONS

➢ Pour 150 ml boiling water over the tea leaves, stir to combine, and strain immediately. You want a strong tea that is not cooked. Allow it to cool after adding the vanilla extract.

➢ In a cocktail shaker, combine the lemon juice, maple syrup, and 50ml of tea. To loosen the egg white, mix it with a fork, then pour 1 tbsp into the shaker. Shake vigorously until the mixture froths. Shake again with a good handful of ice.

➢ Strain twice into an ice-filled glass. Pour 20 ml of water into the glass, followed by 20 ml of pomegranate juice. Allow a few moments for the juice to settle — it will float just underneath the egg white froth.

25. ORANGE MOSCOW MULE MOCKTAIL

Total Time: 5 Mins

Servings: 1

INGREDIENTS

- 1 orange juice
- 1 cup of ice
- 6.8-ounce bottle of non-alcoholic ginger beer
- fresh mint leaves, for garnish

INSTRUCTIONS

➤ Set aside 2 to 3 slices of orange for garnish after quartering it. Put the rest of the orange in a copper cup and juice it (or any glass). Fill the glass to the top with ice. Add the ginger beer and decorate with orange slices and mint leaves.

26. WHISKEY SOUR MOCKTAIL

Total Time: 10 Mins

Servings: 1

INGREDIENTS

- 25ml of lemon juice
- ½ egg white
- ¾ tbsp of sugar syrup, or to taste
- ice cubes
- 1 lemon slice and 1 cocktail cherry, to serve

For the infusion
- 1 tsp Assam tea leaves
- ¼ tsp. vanilla extract

INSTRUCTIONS

➤ Make the infusion first. Pour 150ml of hot water from the kettle over the tea leaves in a heatproof teapot or container. Immediately strain through a fine mesh sieve into a second heatproof jug, discarding the tea leaves, so the tea doesn't become too strong. Allow it to cool before adding the vanilla.

➤ In a cocktail shaker, pour 50ml of the cooled tea infusion, then add the lemon juice, egg white, sugar syrup, and a handful of ice. Shake until the shaker's exterior feels very cold.

➤ To serve, strain the mocktail into an ice-filled tumbler and garnish with a lemon slice and a cocktail cherry.

27. VIRGIN MARGARITA

Total Time: 5 Mins

Servings: 1

INGREDIENTS

- 1 ounce of fresh lime juice
- ½ ounce fresh lemon juice
- ¼ tsp maple syrup or simple syrup
- ⅛ tsp pickle juice (optional but recommended!)
- 3 ounces tonic water
- Lime wheel for the garnish

INSTRUCTIONS

➢ Cut a notch in a lime slice and run it around the rim of a glass. Dip the rim's edge into a flaky sea salt plate (or for a festive look, use Margarita Salt).

➢ Combine the lime juice, lemon juice, maple syrup, and pickle juice in a serving glass. Mix in the ice and tonic water. As a garnish, place a lime wheel on top.

28. VIRGIN MARY MOCKTAIL

Total Time: 5 Mins

Servings: 1

INGREDIENTS

- Lemon or lime wedge for rimming glass
- Choice of seasoning(s) for rimming glass
- 8 ounces of tomato juice
- 2 tsp lemon juice
- 1 tsp lime juice
- 2–3 drops of hot pepper sauce
- ½ tsp Worcestershire sauce
- ½ tsp prepared horseradish

- Dash of freshly ground black pepper
- Desired toppings

INSTRUCTIONS

➢ On a small plate, add about 1 tsp of the seasoning you're using. To moisten the rim of the glass, rub a lemon or lime wedge around it.
➢ To evenly coat the rim of the glass, dip it into the seasoning. Fill a glass with ice.
➢ Fill a cocktail shaker halfway with ice. Tomato juice, lemon juice, lime juice, spicy pepper sauce, Worcestershire sauce, horseradish, and pepper are all good additions.
➢ Cover and vigorously shake for 15 seconds.
➢ Strain into an ice-rimmed glass. Garnish with the desired toppings.

NOTES

1. Adjust ingredients according to your personal taste as needed!

29. VIRGIN MOJITO MOCKTAIL RECIPE

Total Time: 5 Mins

Servings: 1

INGREDIENTS

- 6 mint leaves, plus additional for garnish
- 1 ounce of lime juice
- 1 ounce orgeat syrup or ½ ounce simple syrup
- 4 ounces of soda water or tonic water
- For serving: ice (try clear ice) and mint leaves

INSTRUCTIONS

➢ Mix the mint leaves in a cocktail shaker. Combine the lime juice and orgeat, or simple syrup.
➢ Put ice in the cocktail shaker and shake it until it's cold.
➢ Fill a cup with ice, then strain the drink into the cup. Top off the glass with soda water. Garnish with more mint leaves and ice.

NOTES

1. Orgeat syrup is a non-alcoholic almond syrup that may be used to sweeten cocktails. It has a distinct nutty flavor with a tinge of citrus that is hard to replicate. Orgeat is simple to get by in your local liquor shop or online. Use Mint Simple Syrup to really spice up the minty taste.

30. VIRGIN MANGO ORANGE MOJITO

Total Time: 5 Mins

Servings: 4

INGREDIENTS

- 1 cup of tightly packed fresh mint
- ¼ cup of sugar
- 1 cup of orange juice
- 8 ounces of mango juice
- 1 tbs fresh lime juice
- 12 ounces of seltzer water
- 1 sliced orange
- 2 cups of ice

INSTRUCTIONS

➢ In a pitcher, mix the mint leaves with a muddler or a wide-handled wooden spoon.
➢ Crush the sugar into the mint leaves.
➢ Stir in the liquids to mix.
➢ Add ½ cup of ice to each glass and garnish with orange rings.
➢ Put one cup of virgin mojito over ice.
➢ Serve and enjoy!

31. PINEAPPLE & LIME MOCKTAIL

Total Time :20 Mins

Servings: 4

INGREDIENTS

- 1 tsp clear honey
- Edible gold glitter
- small bunch of coriander leaves
- juice 1 lime
- 750ml of pineapple juice
- a handful of ice
- 400ml of tonic water

INSTRUCTIONS

- ➤ Brush a line of honey down one side of four tumblers using a pastry brush dipped in honey. Sprinkle some edible gold glitter over the honey, then place the cups in the refrigerator.
- ➤ Cut the coriander leaves and combine them with the lime juice, pineapple juice, and ice in a cocktail shaker. Shake until the shaker's outside feels chilly. Strain into glasses, add more ice cubes, then divide 650ml of pineapple juice and tonic water evenly among the glasses.

32. VIRGIN STRAWBERRY DAIQUIRI RECIPE

Total Time: 5 Mins

Servings: 4

INGREDIENTS

- 12 ounces of frozen strawberries
- ¼ cup of simple syrup
- 3 tbsp of freshly squeezed lime juice
- 1 cup of tonic water or lemon-lime soda (Sprite), plus more for serving
- ½ to ¾ cup of water
- 1 cup of ice

INSTRUCTIONS

➤ Combine everything and puree it in a blender until it's smooth, thick puree forms, adding just enough water as needed and stopping and scraping as needed. (All blenders are different, so start at the low end of the water and work up.)

➤ Serve with a splash of lemon-lime soda in each glass if preferred (this can make a more drinkable texture, depending on how much liquid you use). If necessary, decorate with fresh strawberries and lime wheels.

33. NON-ALCOHOLIC JUICY JULEP

Total Time: 5 Mins

Servings: 1

INGREDIENTS

- Ice
- 1 measure pineapple juice
- 1 measure orange juice
- 1 measure freshly squeezed lime juice
- Ginger ale to top it off
- 1 tsp crushed mint
- A sprig of mint as garnish
- Lime wedge or pineapple slice, as garnish

INSTRUCTIONS

➤ Add ice to a tall glass. Combine the pineapple, orange, and lime juices in a bowl. Mix in the mint leaves and top with ginger ale. If preferred, garnish with a sprig of mint, a lime wedge, or a pineapple slice. Serve right away.

34. GRAPEFRUIT GIN SOUR MOCKTAIL

Total Time: 5 Mins

Servings: 2

INGREDIENTS

- ½ red grapefruit, juiced and 2 strips of zest to serve
- 2 tbsp simple sugar syrup
- 50ml non-alcoholic gin
- ½ lemon, juiced
- 1 egg white
- A handful of ice

INSTRUCTIONS

- ➢ First, mix all the ingredients except the ice in a cocktail shaker or a big jam jar with a good seal. To mix, shake thoroughly.
- ➢ Add a handful of ice to shake vigorously for at least 30 seconds, or until the sides of the shaker are cold. Strain into tumblers with extra ice or into coupe glasses without ice. For garnish, use a grapefruit twist.

35. VIRGIN BLOODY MARY

Total Time: 10 Mins

Servings: 4

INGREDIENTS

- 2 cups of chilled tomato juice
- ¼ cup of fresh lemon juice
- 2 tsp of Worcestershire sauce (vegan as desired)
- 2 tsp prepared horseradish
- 2 tsp olive juice (optional)
- ½ tsp Tabasco hot sauce
- ½ tsp celery salt
- ⅛ tsp black pepper
- Ice, for serving (try clear ice!)

- For the rim: Old Bay seasoning (purchased or homemade) and kosher salt
- For the garnish: celery, lemon wedge, olive, cocktail onion (use cocktail picks if desired)

INSTRUCTIONS

➢ Chill the tomato juice if you have time. Before adding the tomato juice, give it a good shake.

➢ Mix the tomato juice, lemon juice, Worcestershire sauce, horseradish, olive juice, Tabasco, celery salt, and black pepper in a large cocktail shaker. To combine, give it a good shake (without ice). Pour into a quart mason jar or a small pitcher to strain.

➢ If you have time, refrigerate the mixture for at least 1 hour or overnight for the best taste. (Or, make it ahead and store it for up to 1 week.) You may, however, serve immediately!

➢ Place half kosher salt and half Old Bay seasoning on a platter to serve (or celery salt). Cut a notch in a lemon wedge and use it to run around the rim of a glass. In a plate of salt, dip the rim's edge.

➢ 1/2 cup of virgin Bloody Mary mix in each glass, gently stirred to combine. Add ice to the glass and the garnishes.

36. SPARKLING PEACH PUNCH

Prep Time: 15 Mins

Cook Time: 2 Mins

Total Time: 17 Mins

Servings: 2

INGREDIENTS

- One 29 ounce. can peaches in syrup, not drained
- 3 cups of water
- 1 ½ cups of sugar
- One 3-ounce package peach flavor gelatin (Jell-0)
- 5 cups of peach juice blend
- ½ cup of lemon juice
- 2 liters of chilled ginger ale

INSTRUCTIONS

- ➢ Puree the peaches in a blender until completely smooth. Place aside.
- ➢ In a large saucepan, combine the water, sugar, and gelatin and bring to a boil, constantly stirring until the sugar and gelatin dissolve. Combine pureed peaches, peach juice blend, and lemon juice in an extra-large bowl. To combine, just mix everything.
- ➢ Chill for 8 hours or until stiff, dividing the mixture into two big freezer bags. May freeze for up to a month.
- ➢ Remove 1-2 frozen bags from the freezer and set aside for 1 hour until ready to serve. Break it into chunks with a fork and pour it into punch bowls or pitchers. 1 liter of ginger ale is added to each container of frozen peach mixture. Stir until slushy, then serve right away.
- ➢ Garnish with sliced peaches, lemons, and mint, if desired.

NOTES

1. Any juice made with peaches will work well. I used a mango-peach juice combination. Prep time does not include freezing time, as this will vary between individuals.

37. PEAR, PUMPKIN & GINGER JUICE MOCKTAIL

Total Time: 10 Mins

Servings: 2

INGREDIENTS

- Tube of black icing
- 50g peeled and deseeded pumpkin or butternut squash
- 1 ripe pear
- 250ml orange juice
- 1cm thick slice ginger

INSTRUCTIONS

➢ Decorate 2 tumblers to look like Halloween pumpkins using the tube of black icing. Pipe triangles for the eyes and noses and zigzags for the mouths. Allow to dry out Cut the pumpkin into smaller pieces and combine it with the pear, orange juice, ginger, and 100ml of cool water in a mixer. Mix until smooth, then pour into the ready glasses.

38. MARGARITA & MORE!

Total Time: 5 Mins

Servings: 1

INGREDIENTS

- 1 ounce of fresh lime juice
- ½ ounce of fresh lemon juice
- ¼ tsp of maple syrup or simple syrup
- ⅛ tsp pickle juice (optional but recommended!)
- 3 ounces of tonic water
- For the garnish: lime wheel, clear ice

INSTRUCTIONS

➢ Notch a lime wedge and then run it around the rim of a glass. The rim is dipped into a platter of flaky sea salt (or for a festive look, use Margarita Salt).
➢ Mix the lime juice, lemon juice, maple syrup, and pickle juice in the serving glass. Add ice and tonic water. Serve garnished with a lime wheel.

39. NON-ALCOHOLIC WHITE SANGRIA RECIPE

Prep Time: 15 Mins

Total Time: 1 Hr 15 Mins

Servings: 48

INGREDIENTS

- 1 large sliced lemon
- 1 large sliced orange
- 5-7 large sliced strawberries
- 10-15 green grapes
- 8-10 sprigs of fresh mint, plus more for garnish
- 20 blueberries
- 12 ounces of white grape juice
- 12 ounces of orange juice
- 24 ounces of sparkling water
- additional fruit for garnish if desired

INSTRUCTIONS

- ➤ Wash and dry all of the fruit.
- ➤ Slice the strawberries, lemon, and orange into thin slices.
- ➤ In a large pitcher, combine the lemon slices, orange slices, strawberries, grapes, blueberries, and mint.
- ➤ Over the fruit, pour the grape juice, orange juice, and sparkling water.
- ➤ Stir well.
- ➤ Before serving, let it chill for one hour.
- ➤ Garnish with fresh mint and fruit in clear glasses.

40. POMEGRANATE MOJITO MOCKTAIL

Total Time: 10 Mins

Servings: 8

INGREDIENTS

- 3 tbsp pomegranate seeds
- big bunch mint
- 2 limes, quartered, plus slices to garnish
- 1l pomegranate juice
- 500ml lemonade

INSTRUCTIONS

- ➤ Divide the pomegranate seeds among the holes in an ice cube tray a day ahead of time, top up with water, and freeze.
- ➤ Set aside half of the mint for serving and toss the remainder into a large jug with the lime quarters. Bash the mint and lime with a rolling pin to release the flavors. Combine the pomegranate juice and lemonade in a pitcher. Place ice cubes in each glass, then pour the pomegranate mixture through a fine strainer over the ice. Serve with lime slices and more mint as garnish.

41. VIRGIN RASPBERRY MANGO MARGARITA SLUSHIES

Total Time: 20 Mins

Servings: 2

INGREDIENTS

For the mango layer

- 2 cups of frozen mango
- ¾ cup of coconut water
- ¼ cup of lime juice
- 2 tsp honey

For the raspberry layer

- 2 cups of frozen raspberries
- ¾ cup of coconut water
- ¼ cup of lime juice
- 2 tsp honey

INSTRUCTIONS

- ➢ To make the mango layer, in a blender, combine frozen mango, coconut water, lime juice, and honey. Mix until smooth, then pour half of the mixture into each glass.
- ➢ To make the raspberry layer, in a blender, combine frozen raspberries, coconut water, lime juice, and honey. Mix until smooth, then pour the mixture into each glass.
- ➢ Serve with lime wedges as a garnish.

42. WATERMELON LIME MOCKTAILS

Total Time: 5 Mins

Servings: 4

INGREDIENTS

- 4 cups of chopped frozen watermelon (cut into 1-inch cubes)
- 2 fresh limes (plus extra lime slices for garnish)
- 1 cup of water
- Seasoning (for rimming the glasses)

INSTRUCTIONS

- ➢ Rim the glasses. In a shallow little plate, place some seasoning. Drizzle a lime wedge along the rims of your serving glasses, then lightly dip the rims in seasoning. Place the glasses in a safe place until you're ready to use them.
- ➢ Blend. In a blender, combine the frozen watermelon pieces, lime juice, and water. Cover and mix until smooth, adding extra water if necessary to get the blender started and obtain a thick slushie consistency.
- ➢ Serve. Pour the mixture into your serving glasses, garnish with a lime slice if preferred, then serve and enjoy!

NOTES

1. Tips for freezing watermelon: I recommend chopping the fresh watermelon into 1-inch cubes to prevent the sliced watermelon from freezing in one big clump (or sticking to your bowl). Then, on a parchment-lined baking tray, arrange the cubes in an equal layer and freeze for at least 2 hours.

43. NEGRONI MOCKTAIL

Prep Time: 10 Mins

Cook Time: 5 Mins

Total Time: 15 Mins

Servings: 1

INGREDIENTS

For the syrup base

- ½ grapefruit
- 1 slice orange
- 125g caster sugar
- 3 lightly crushed cardamom pods
- A pinch of coriander seeds
- A few drops of red food coloring

For the cocktail

- ice
- 25ml of white grape juice
- 1 slice of orange (optional)

INSTRUCTIONS

➢ Cut the grapefruit into small slices and combine with the orange slice, sugar, 125ml water, cardamom pods, and coriander seeds in a pan. Warm the mixture to a low simmer and cook for about 5 minutes, smashing the fruit with the back of a wooden spoon as it softens to release the juices. Remove the fruit from the fire after it has softened and the white pith has vanished and set it aside to cool. You can add a dab of red food coloring to the syrup if desired.

> Strain the syrup mixture when it has cooled, discarding the spices and fruit fragments. Pour 25ml of syrup, grape juice, and ice into a glass.

44. TRIPLE BERRY SPARKLERS

Prep Time: 4 Hrs

Cook Time: 15 Mins

Total Time: 4 Hrs 15 Mins

Servings: 6

INGREDIENTS

For the berry ice cubes

- 1 ¼ cups of coconut water
- ⅓ cup of blueberries
- ⅓ cup of raspberries
- ⅓ cup of chopped strawberries

For the drink

- 2 tbsp honey
- 2 tbsp freshly squeezed lime juice
- 2 tbsp freshly squeezed lemon juice
- 12-ounce cans of seltzer

INSTRUCTIONS

Make berry ice cubes

> Put blueberries, raspberries, and strawberries in an ice tray, then add coconut water and make berry ice cubes. Freeze for 4 hours until completely solid.
> Make drink: Mix honey with lime and lemon juices in a pitcher or big measuring cup. Stir in the honey until it is fully dissolved. Stir in the seltzer until combined.
> Ice the serving glasses, then fill them with the lemon-lime combination.

45. CRANBERRY MOCKTAIL

Total Time: 10 Mins

Servings: 8

INGREDIENTS

- 3 cups of cranberry pomegranate juice or 2 cups of cranberry and 1 cup of pomegranate juice
- 6 cups of club soda
- ½ cup of lime juice or the juice of 4 limes
- ¼ cup of mint leaves
- Garnishes
- ¼ cup of cranberries, fresh or frozen
- ¼ cup of pomegranate seeds or 1 pomegranate
- 1 lime sliced into wedges
- 8 sprigs of mint

INSTRUCTIONS

➢ Fill a pitcher with pomegranate and cranberry juice. Put club soda in. To combine, stir.
➢ Juice from three limes, squeezed. To the pitcher, add the lime juice. To combine, stir.
➢ Mix in fresh cranberries, pomegranate seeds, mint leaves, and 2 to 3 cups of ice. To combine, stir.
➢ Add ice to each cup individually. Add the mocktail. Add some fresh cranberries, pomegranate seeds, a lime wedge, and a mint sprig on the top. Enjoy!

NOTES

1. Use fresh cranberries and pomegranates to give each drink a festive feel.
2. Use club soda instead of tonic water. Since you're using juice, there's no need for the additional sugar that tonic water contains.
3. Just before serving, prepare the pitcher and add the ice. The drink will get diluted when the ice melts. Or, add the ice to each serving, so it doesn't get too watered down.
4. Use fresh lime juice; a juicer will help you get all of the juice from each lime.

46. BLUE LAGOON MOCKTAIL

Total Time: 5 Mins

Servings: 1

INGREDIENTS

- ¼ cup of blue Curaçao syrup
- 2 tbsp of freshly squeezed lemon juice
- 12 Fl ounces of lemon-lime soda such as Sprite
- lemon slice for garnish
- Ice optional

INSTRUCTIONS

➤ Use a citrus reamer to squeeze the juice from a fresh lemon.
➤ If preferred, add two or three ice cubes to a 15-ounce highball glass.
➤ Pour the blue Curaçao syrup and lemon juice into the glass, and then slowly fill the rest of the glass with Sprite. To combine, gently stir.
➤ Add a paper straw and a lemon slice as garnishes. Enjoy right now.

NOTES

1. Dip the glasses in water, then sugar, to coat the rims.
2. Chill the Sprite and blue Curaçao syrup to reduce the need for ice.
3. By chilling the drink in a freezer-safe container for 4-6 hours, you can turn it into a slushie. Halfway through, mix it. A fork may be used to break up any large clumps in the drink before serving.

47. HALLOWEEN MOCKTAIL PUNCH

Total Time: 10 Mins

Servings: 14-15

INGREDIENTS

- 425g can lychees
- 225g jar cocktail cherries
- 15 raisins
- 1-liter chilled carton of blueberry, blackberry or purple grape juice
- 1-liter chilled carton of cherry or cranberry juice
- 1-liter of chilled sparkling water
- 2 pairs of powder-free disposable gloves

INSTRUCTIONS

➤ Use water to fill each of the disposable gloves. Use a bag clip or a knot to tie the top of each like you would a balloon. Freeze overnight.

➤ Drain the cocktail cherries and lychees, saving the juices in a jug. To make "eyeballs," insert a raisin onto the end of each cherry before inserting the cherries into the lychees.

➤ Using the 'eyeballs', add all of the juices and the saved lychee and cherry juices to a big bowl. To serve, carefully remove the gloves from the frozen hands and stir them into the punch.

48. BLACKBERRY VIRGIN MOJITO

Prep Time: 10 Mins

Total Time: 40 Mins

Servings: 4

INGREDIENTS

For mint syrup

- ½ cup of packed fresh mint leaves
- 1 cup of granulated sugar
- 1 cup of water

For mojito

- 1 cup of blackberries
- 1 tsp granulated sugar
- ½ cup of lime juice
- Ice
- 12-ounce seltzer
- Fresh mint, for garnish

INSTRUCTIONS

- ➢ Crush mint leaves in a small saucepan with a wooden spoon or in a mortar and pestle. Bring sugar and water to a boil in a medium saucepan while stirring constantly to ensure that the sugar is completely dissolved. Allow the water to simmer for a further 3 minutes. Let the mixture to reach room temperature, then strain off the mint leaves using a wooden spoon to help remove all of the liquid from the leaves.
- ➢ Add blackberries and sugar to a small bowl, and with a wooden spoon, crush the blackberries until they are finely ground.
- ➢ Add 2 tsp of simple syrup and 2 tbsp of lime juice into each of the four glasses with the blackberries. Fill the glasses with ice, then add seltzer and mint.

49. SPICY GRAPEFRUIT GINGER FIZZ MOCKTAIL

Total Time: 5 Mins

Servings: 1

INGREDIENTS

- ½ cup of 100% grapefruit juice
- 1 tbsp fresh lime juice
- 1 sprig of fresh mint
- 1-3 slices of fresh jalapeno
- 1 cup of ice
- ½ cup of non-alcoholic ginger beer

INSTRUCTIONS

➤ Muddle the lime and jalapeno. In a cocktail shaker, mix the grapefruit juice, lime juice, mint, and jalapeno slices. Gently stir the mint and jalapenos into the juices using a muddler or wooden spoon.

➤ Combine. In a large cocktail glass or copper mug, put the ice. Over the ice, strain the grapefruit juice combination. Add the ginger beer on top and mix it up gently.

➤ Serve with a garnish. Enjoy the drink after adding a jalapeno, extra citrus slice, or fresh mint sprig as a garnish. Cheers!

Notes

➤ Grapefruit juice and ginger beer: To keep this drink nice and tart and not too sweet, as mentioned above, I suggest using 100% pure grapefruit juice and a kind of ginger beer with a low sugar content.

➤ If you don't have a cocktail shaker, muddle the juices in a mason jar or a glass, then strain them into your serving glass.

50. CLEMENTINE MOCK MOJITO

Total Time: 5 Mins

Servings: 1

INGREDIENTS

- 1 clementine
- ½ tsp demerara sugar
- 1 chopped lemon wedge
- ice
- small handful of mint, woody stalks removed
- A few drops of orange blossom water
- sparkling water to top up

INSTRUCTIONS

- ➢ Half of the clementine is juiced, while the other half is cut into little pieces. Add the sugar after pouring the juice into a glass. Add the clementine and lemon, then use a muddler to crush.
- ➢ Add some ice cubes, mint, and orange blossom. Slowly top with sparkling water.

51. STRAWBERRY LEMONADE

Prep Time: 5 Mins

Cook Time: 20 Mins

Total Time: 25 Mins

Servings: 6

INGREDIENTS

- 1 cup of granulated sugar
- 6 cups of water, divided
- 1 hulled and halved pound of strawberries
- 1 cup of freshly squeezed lemon juice
- Ice
- Mint leaves (optional)

INSTRUCTIONS

> ➢ Sugar and one cup of water are combined in a small saucepan over medium heat. Bring to a boil and simmer until dissolved. Let cool.
> ➢ Strawberries and one cup of water are mixed in a blender. Blend until pureed. Remove any remaining solids from the puree using a fine-mesh strainer.
> ➢ Mix the simple syrup, strawberry puree, lemon juice, and the other 4 cups of water in a large pitcher. To suit your tastes, add extra water or lemon juice.
> ➢ If preferred, serve it over ice with mint.

52. APPLETINI MOCKTAIL RECIPE

Total Time: 5 Mins

Servings: 2

INGREDIENTS

- 3 ounces of apple juice
- 2 ounces of lemon juice fresh-squeezed is best
- 2 ounces granny smith apple syrup
- ice cubes

INSTRUCTIONS

> ➢ In a cocktail shaker or mixing cup, combine 3 ounces of apple juice, 2 ounces of lemon juice, and 2 ounces of granny smith apple syrup.
> ➢ Add a few ice cubes.
> ➢ Stir or shake until well combined and chilled.
> ➢ Then strain into martini glasses.

NOTES

To make a big batch

1. Mix 3 cups of apple juice, 2 cups of lemon juice, and 2 cups of granny smith syrup in a pitcher.
2. Stir everything together.
3. Refrigerate until ready to serve. Don't add ice since it dilutes the taste.
4. Slices or wedges of Granny Smith apples are used as a garnish in addition to green rimming sugar.

53. BEASTLY BLACKBERRY & BAY LEMONADE MOCKTAIL

Cook Time: 7 Mins

Prep Time: 5 Mins

Total Time: 12 Mins

Servings: 4

INGREDIENTS

- 3-bay leaves
- 50g golden caster sugar
- 1 lemon
- 200g blackberries
- 300ml sparkling water

To garnish
- lychees
- green olives

INSTRUCTIONS

➢ Place the bay leaves, 350 ml of water, and golden caster sugar in a pan. Bring it to a boil, turn off the heat, and let it cool. Remove and discard the bay leaves. Put the chunks of lemon into a blender. Blend in the blackberries (fresh or defrosted) and the bay leaf infusion, then drain into a jug through a sieve to get rid of the pith and seeds. Pour the sparkling water into tumblers or wine glasses and serve if you want to decorate the drink. Stuff lychees with green olives and skewer them onto cocktail sticks.

54. JUNETEENTH PUNCH

Total Time: 5 Mins

Servings: 20

INGREDIENTS

- 6 cups of cranberry juice
- 1 L chilled ginger ale or 7Up
- 4 cup of pineapple juice
- 4 cup of orange juice
- ¼ cup of lemon or lime juice
- ½ gal strawberry sorbet
- 1 sliced navel orange
- 1 cup of pineapple chunks or rings
- Maraschino cherries
- Sliced strawberries

INSTRUCTIONS

- ➢ Mix the cranberry juice, pineapple juice, orange juice, lemon juice, and ginger ale in a large punch bowl. Decorate with fresh fruit and sorbet.
- ➢ Immediately serve in cold glasses.

55. HURRICANE MOCKTAIL

Total Time: 5 Mins

Servings: 1

INGREDIENTS

- 2 Ounces fresh orange juice
- 2 Ounces 100% no-sugar-added pineapple juice
- 2 Ounces sweet and sour mix
- ½ Ounces simple syrup
- ¼ Ounce grenadine syrup
- 2 Ounces Passion-fruit-flavored sparkling water
- Pineapple wedge, with pineapple leaves, for garnish

INSTRUCTIONS

➤ Mix orange juice, pineapple juice, sweet and sour mix, simple syrup, and grenadine in a cocktail shaker filled with ice. Wrap tightly and shake. Into a 10-ounce martini glass, strain. Add sparkling water with a passion fruit taste on top. Now garnish with a pineapple slice and pineapple leaves if desired.

56. WHIPPED LEMONADE

Total Time: 10 Mins

Servings: 4

INGREDIENTS

- 1 cup of lemonade
- ½ cup of sweetened condensed milk
- Juice of 1 lemon
- 4 cups of ice
- Lemon slices, for garnish

INSTRUCTIONS

➤ Mix all the ingredients in a blender until they are smooth and creamy. Add more ice to thicken as desired.

➤ Pour into glasses before serving, then top with a lemon slice.

57. NON-ALCOHOLIC MARGARITA

Total Time: 4 Hrs 15 Mins

Servings: 2

INGREDIENTS

- ⅔ cup of fresh lime juice
- ⅓ cup of fresh orange juice
- ⅓ cup of light agave syrup
- Kosher salt
- 1 cup of ice cubes
- 1 cup of chilled lime seltzer

INSTRUCTIONS

Special equipment

➤ a 12-compartment ice cube tray

➤ In a measuring cup with a spout, mix the lime juice, orange juice, and agave. Pour into a 12-part ice cube tray, then freeze for at least 4 hours, or even overnight, until the mixture is solid.

➤ Put some salt in a little bowl. Dip the rims of two glasses in water, then in the salt to coat.

➤ Mix on high until smooth and pourable after adding the ice cubes, seltzer, and frozen juice cubes to a blender. Pour it into the ready glasses and start serving right away.

58. STRAWBERRY CUCUMBER MOJITO MOCKTAIL

Total Time: 5 Mins

Servings: 2

INGREDIENTS

- 6 large strawberries, tops removed
- 6 fresh mint leaves
- 4-6 slices cucumber
- 2 packets (True Lime)
- 1 can of sparkling water
- 2 tsp sweetener of choice, if desired, (simple syrup, agave syrup, or date syrup)

INSTRUCTIONS

➢ First, crush your strawberries and mint in a bowl until totally mashed. In two glasses, divide the strawberry-mint combination. Add ice to each cup.
➢ Add two cucumbers to each glass, then fill them with sparkling water to the top. Add 1 True Lime packet and any sweetener to each drink (if using). Stir well.
➢ Serve and enjoy!

59. PERFECT ARNOLD PALMER

Total Time: 45 Mins

Servings: 8

INGREDIENTS

For the lemonade

- 3 cups of divided water
- ¾ cup of granulated sugar
- Juice of 6 large lemons

For the tea

- 4 cups of water
- ⅓ cup of honey
- 5 black tea bags

- Ice
- Fresh mint
- Lemon wedges

INSTRUCTIONS

- ➢ To make lemonade, heat 1 cup of water and sugar in a small saucepan over medium heat while stirring to dissolve the sugar. Boil for 2 minutes. Allow cool to room temperature.
- ➢ Combine the remaining 2 cups of water, the simple syrup, and the lemon juice.
- ➢ To make tea, heat the water in a medium pot over medium-high heat. Stir in the honey to dissolve it. Turn off the heat and then add the tea bags. Allow it to steep for 5 minutes. Let it cool to room temperature.
- ➢ Combine tea and lemonade in a big pitcher. Pour into glasses over ice, top with mint, and add lemon slices as garnish.

60. TEA-TINI MOCKTAIL

Prep Time: 15 Mins

Cook Time: 25 Mins

Total Time: 40 Mins

Servings: 1-2

INGREDIENTS

- Ice
- 6 ounces of unsweetened iced tea
- 3 ounces of Lemon Simple Syrup
- 1 strip of lemon zest, sliced with a vegetable peeler

Lemon Simple Syrup
- 1 lemon, juiced
- 1 cup of sugar

INSTRUCTIONS

➢ Add a handful of ice to a cocktail shaker. Shake in the tea and the simple lemon syrup. Pour into a chilled martini glass. Add a lemon strip as a garnish.

Lemon Simple Syrup

➢ In a small saucepan, mix 1 cup each of water and sugar. Boil for a few minutes, then turn down the heat and simmer for another 10 min. Allow to cool, then mix in lemon juice. Use right away or store in the freezer, covered.

61. RAINBOW COCONUT WATER SPRITZERS

Total Time: 15 Mins

Servings: 8

INGREDIENTS

Handfuls of fresh

- raspberries
- strawberries
- cherries
- peaches
- pineapple
- Lime slices
- Fresh mint
- blueberries
- blackberries
- 8 ounces of coconut-or vanilla-flavored seltzer water
- 16 ounces of coconut water

INSTRUCTIONS

➢ Add a little amount of crushed ice to each glass before adding the rainbow-colored fruit. Once the fruit is in the glasses, top them over with ice and approximately 4 ounces of coconut water each.
➢ Serve each with a splash of flavored seltzer. Add more fresh mint as a garnish.

62. PINEAPPLE-MINT MOJITO MOCKTAIL

Total Time: 3 Mins

Servings: 1

INGREDIENTS

- 2 packets of No Calorie Sweetener
- ¼ cup of pineapple juice
- 10 sprigs of fresh mint, plus more for garnish
- 1 lime, juiced
- ½ cup of club soda

INSTRUCTIONS

➢ In a cocktail shaker, muddle mint leaves with No Calorie Sweetener.
➢ Mix the pineapple juice, lime juice, and ice for 15 seconds. Strained into a tall glass of ice and top with club soda. Add a mint sprig as a garnish.

63. VIRGIN MARYS

Total Time: 10 Mins

Servings: 6

INGREDIENTS

- 3 stalks of celery from the heart, including leaves, plus extra for serving
- 2 tsp prepared horseradish
- 1 tsp chopped shallot
- Dash Worcestershire sauce
- 1 tsp celery salt
- 1 tsp kosher salt
- 12 dashes of hot sauce, or to taste
- 2 limes, juiced
- 48-ounce of tomato juice

INSTRUCTIONS

➤ To puree the celery, cut it into large pieces, including the leaves, and place them in the steel-bladed food processor bowl. Process the horseradish, shallot, Worcestershire sauce, celery salt, kosher salt, Tabasco, and lime juice until well combined. Pour the mixture into a big pitcher, then pour in the tomato juice.

➤ Pour into tall glasses and top each serving with the celery stalk's top.

64. HIBISCUS ICED TEA SPARKLER

Prep Time: 5 Mins

Cook Time: 55 Mins

Total Time: 1 Hr

Servings: 4

INGREDIENTS

- 4 cups of boiling water
- 8 bags of hibiscus tea
- ½ cup of honey
- ice
- 2 cups of sparkling water
- ¼ cup of mint leaves
- strawberries for garnish

INSTRUCTIONS

➤ Depending on your preference for tea strength, add tea bags, honey, and boiling water in a big pitcher. Steep for 30 to 1 hour.

➤ Remove the tea bags.

➤ Add ice to a pitcher, then mix in sparkling water.

➤ Add mint.

➤ Refrigerate for 1 hour or until chilled.

➤ Garnish with strawberries.

➤ Serve.

65. SPARKLING TROPICAL MOCK-TAIL

Perp Time: 5 Mins

Servings: 4

INGREDIENTS

- ¾ cup of pineapple juice
- ½ cup of mango juice
- ¼ cup of fresh lime juice
- 8 ounces of non-alcoholic ginger beer
- Pineapple wedges, for garnish
- Mango slices for garnish

INSTRUCTIONS

➤ Combine the pineapple, mango, and lime juices in a cocktail shaker with ice. Shake vigorously. Strain into highball glasses filled with ice. Add some ginger beer on top of each. Serve right away with pineapple slices and mango wedges as garnish.

66. NEW MOTHER MOCKTAIL

Total Time: 5 Mins

Servings: 12

INGREDIENTS

- 32 ounces of apple juice
- 32 ounces of cranberry juice
- 32 ounces of orange juice
- Crushed ice
- Orange slices for garnish

INSTRUCTIONS

➤ Add the juice and stir to combine in a large pitcher or punch bowl. If your bowl or pitcher holds less than 96 ounces, mix the juices in a lesser quantity in equal parts and refill as needed.
➤ If preferred, serve over ice and garnish with orange wedges.

67. VIRGIN CRANBERRY BASIL SANGRIA

Total Time: 10 Mins

Servings: 4

INGREDIENTS

- 3 cups of cranberry juice
- ½ cup of orange Juice
- 12-ounce seltzer
- 1 sliced orange
- 1 cored and sliced apple
- ⅓ cup of frozen cranberries
- ¼ cup of packed basil leaves
- Ice

INSTRUCTIONS

- ➢ Combine the cranberry juice, orange juice, and seltzer in a big pitcher. Add the fruit and basil and mix thoroughly.
- ➢ Pour to serve over ice.

68. CHOCOLATE MARTINI

Prep Time: 5 Mins

Servings: 2

INGREDIENTS

- 1 cup of cold milk
- ¼ cup of best-quality chocolate syrup, plus more for dipping rims
- 1 tbsp corn syrup
- Crushed ice, as needed
- 2 martini glasses
- Chocolate sprinkles

INSTRUCTIONS

➢ Combine the milk, ¼ cup of chocolate syrup, corn syrup, and crushed ice in a mixture and mix until smooth.

➢ Pour some chocolate syrup over one small plate and some of the chocolate sprinkles onto another small plate. Dip each glass's rim in the chocolate syrup, then in the chocolate sprinkles. Pour the chocolate-milk mixture into each glass to the top.

69. SPARKLING BERRY AND POMEGRANATE

Total Time: 5 Mins

Servings: 4

INGREDIENTS

- Two 12-ounce cans of chilled Sparkling Berry Water
- 4 ounces of pomegranate juice
- cranberries to garnish
- fresh thyme to garnish

INSTRUCTIONS

➢ Add ½ can sparkling water, 1 ounce of pomegranate juice, and 2-3 cranberries to a highball glass. Garnish with 1-2 sprigs of thyme and serve.

➢ Four mocktails will be made. Enjoy!

70. POPSICLE PUNCH

Total Time: 10 Mins

Servings: 6

INGREDIENTS

- 4 cups of lemon-lime soda
- 4 cups of lemonade
- 12-ounce seltzer
- 1 cup of sliced strawberries, plus more garnish
- 2 mangoes, cubed, plus more for garnish
- 3 Strawberry Fruit Pops
- 3 Mango Fruit Pops

INSTRUCTIONS

➢ Combine the Coke, lemonade, seltzer, strawberries, and mangoes in a large pitcher. Pour into glasses and decorate with strawberry and mango slices on the rim. As a garnish, add a popsicle.

71. CRANBERRY-LIME MOCKTAIL

Prep Time: 20 Mins

Cook Time: 40 Mins

Total Time: 1 Hr

Servings: 6-8

INGREDIENTS

- 2 cups of fresh or frozen cranberries, plus more, for serving
- 1 ¼ cups of sugar
- ¾ cup of frozen limeade concentrate
- ½ cup of fresh lime juice, plus lime slices, for serving
- Seltzer, for serving

INSTRUCTIONS

- ➢ In a medium saucepan over high heat, combine the cranberries, sugar, and 1 cup of water. Bring to a boil, then reduce to low heat. Smash the cranberries with a potato masher, then boil for 10 minutes, or until slightly reduced and dark red. Allow it to cool for 10 minutes.
- ➢ Strain the mixture into a heat safe container through a strainer, pushing on the cranberry solids to extract all of the juice. Allow to cool for 30 minutes.
- ➢ In a pitcher, stir together the cranberry syrup, limeade, and lime juice.
- ➢ Combine equal parts of drink mix and seltzer. Serve with cranberries and a lime slice over ice.

72. CARAMEL APPLE PIE MOCKTAIL

Total Time: 25 Mins

Servings: 6

INGREDIENTS

- 6 cups of apple cider
- ½ cup of caramel syrup
- 3 cups of sparkling water
- 2 tsp cinnamon
- 2 apples
- Rosemary sprigs, around 6
- Golden brown sugar for rimming

INSTRUCTIONS

- ➢ Combine the apple cider, caramel syrup, and cinnamon in a pitcher.
- ➢ Add the apple pieces, which have been thinly sliced, to the pitcher. After adding the rosemary, wait for 20 minutes.
- ➢ Pour the sparkling water into the pitcher when the 20 minutes have gone. Mix.
- ➢ Then, use the golden-brown sugar to rim the glasses.
- ➢ Fill the cups with the mocktail made with caramel apple pie.

73. APPLE CIDER SLUSHIES

Total Time: 2 Hrs 30 Mins

Servings: 2

INGREDIENTS

- 3 cups of apple cider
- 1 lemon, juiced
- ½ tsp ground cinnamon
- 2 mini cinnamon-sugar doughnuts

INSTRUCTIONS

➤ In a loaf pan, stir together the cider, lemon juice, and cinnamon. 1 hour in the freezer.

➤ Take the cider mixture from the freezer and scrape the slushy mixture with a fork to prevent it from turning into a giant ice cube. Return it to the freezer for another hour after fully scraping and stirring.

➤ Take the cider mixture from the freezer and scrape and mix it with a fork until it has the consistency of shaved ice. If it's not frozen enough for you, return it to the fridge for another 45 minutes. Otherwise, spoon into two glasses and decorate with a tiny doughnut on each rim.

74. MERMAID REFRESHER

Prep Time: 5 Mins

Servings: 1

INGREDIENTS

- ½ cup of seltzer
- ½ cup of blue punch
- 2 tbsp of pineapple juice
- 2 tbsp lemonade
- 1 maraschino cherry, for garnish
- 1 lemon slice, for garnish

INSTRUCTIONS

- ➢ 1 cocktail umbrella
- ➢ Stir the seltzer, blue punch, pineapple juice, and lemonade in a cup. Skewer the cherry and lemon slices on a cocktail umbrella and place them on top of the drink.

75. RASPBERRY MINT LIMEADE

Prep Time: 5 Mins

Cook Time: 10 Mins

Total Time: 15 Mins

Servings: 6

INGREDIENTS

- 2 cups of frozen raspberries
- 1 ½ cups of water
- ¼ cup of cane sugar
- 8 mint sprigs, plus more for garnish
- 1 cup of freshly squeezed lime juice
- 3 cups of soda water

INSTRUCTIONS

- ➢ In a saucepan, combine frozen raspberries. Stir the water and sugar to a boil over medium-high heat, then reduce to medium. Simmer for 5 minutes, stirring occasionally, until the berries are very soft and almost dissolved. Remove the pan from the heat after stirring in the mint sprigs. Allow to cool before removing the mint. To make a thicker beverage, puree it in a blender or immersion blender. Strain and discard solids for a smoother texture. Mix in the lime juice.
- ➢ Divide the juice among the six glasses, then add the soda water and mint leaves on top.

76. BRAZILIAN LEMONADE RECIPE

Total Time: 10 Mins

Servings: 4

INGREDIENTS

- 3 limes
- ⅓ cup of sugar
- 3 cups of water
- 3 tbsp sweetened condensed milk
- Ice

INSTRUCTIONS

- ➢ Wash and quarter the limes, then combine them with the sugar, water, and sweetened condensed milk in a blender. Pulse the limes until they are finely chopped, then run the fluid through a strainer to get the pulp and peel out of it.
- ➢ Serve the juice over ice or combine it with ice for a slushy-like consistency.

77. ROSE LEMON SPRITZER

Total Time: 5 Mins

Servings: 1

INGREDIENTS

- 2 tbsp rose water optional
- 2 tbsp of fresh lemon juice
- 1-2 tbsp of honey or to taste (use agave if vegan)
- a few drops of blood orange or pomegranate juice for color (optional)
- ¾ cup of sparkling water or more to taste
- fresh roses for garnish (optional)

INSTRUCTIONS

- ➢ Mix all the rose water, fresh lemon juice, honey, and blood orange or pomegranate juice in a cocktail shaker with ice (if using). Shake all ingredients together, then strain into a glass. the sparkling water in. Add fresh flowers as a garnish. DRINK!

78. MOCK COLADA

Prep Time: 5 Mins

Servings: 1

INGREDIENTS

- 2 tbsp of freshly squeezed lime juice
- ½ cup of pineapple juice
- 2 tbsp of coconut milk
- 1 tbsp honey
- ¼ cup of coconut-flavor seltzer
- 2 maraschino cherries
- 2 small wedges of fresh pineapple

INSTRUCTIONS

➢ Combine the lime juice, pineapple juice, coconut milk, honey, and 3 to 4 ice cubes in a cocktail shaker. To cool the beverage and dissolve the honey, cover and shake. Strain into a hurricane glass with 15 to 20 ounces of crushed ice. Add the seltzer to the top. On a cocktail pick, garnish with maraschino cherries and pineapple wedges.

79. SPARKLING CRANBERRY LIME MOCKTAIL

Total Time: 5 Mins

Servings: 2

INGREDIENTS

- One 10-ounce bag of frozen cranberries or 1 bag of fresh cranberries
- 1 cup of water
- 1 cup of granulated sugar
- Two 12-ounce cans of Sparkling Lime
- Optional: additional frozen cranberries and a twist of lime wedges for garnish

INSTRUCTIONS

- ➢ Cranberry Simple Syrup
- ➢ Blend or process frozen cranberries until finely chopped after defrosting.
- ➢ Cook water, sugar, and cranberries in a medium saucepan over medium heat until the sugar dissolves. About 2 minutes.
- ➢ Remove the mixture from the heat and press the cranberry pieces out of the mixture using a cheesecloth or small strainer.
- ➢ Keep the remaining liquid in the refrigerator in a covered container.
- ➢ This syrup may be stored for up to a week.
- ➢ Cranberry-Lime Sparkling Cocktail
- ➢ If preferred, add about ¼ cup of frozen cranberries to each of the two highball glasses along with the ice.
- ➢ To each glass, add 2 tsp of simple cranberry syrup.
- ➢ Put Sparkling Lime in glasses.
- ➢ Sugared cranberries and a lime twist serve as garnish.

80. NON-ALCOHOLIC SANGRIA

Total Time: 20 Mins

Servings: 10

INGREDIENTS

- 4 cups of white grape juice
- ¼ cup of blueberries
- ¾ cup of blueberries
- 1 cup of orange juice
- Juice from 1 lime + 2 limes
- 2 oranges
- 2 bananas
- 2 peaches

INSTRUCTIONS

- ➢ Combine ¼ cup of blueberries and white grape juice in a blender. Put a bowl or jar with this liquid mixture in.
- ➢ Add the juices of the orange and lime. Stir well to combine.

➤ ¾ cup of blueberries, two oranges, two bananas, two limes, and the liquid mixture are placed in a container with ice. For about two hours, let the sangria stand in the refrigerator.

81. PURPLE PUNCH

Total Time: 5 Mins

Servings: 1

INGREDIENTS

- 5 mint leaves, plus more for garnish
- 6 blueberries, plus more for garnish
- 3 lemon wheels, plus more for garnish
- ice
- Red Bull Purple Edition Sugar free
- Lemonade

INSTRUCTIONS

➤ Mix mint, blueberries, and lemon wheels in a glass. Add ice. Stir with a bar spoon. 4 parts Red Bull Purple Edition sugar free to 1 part fresh lemonade, or 8ounce Red Bull Purple Edition sugar free to 2ounces fresh lemonade. Add extra mint leaves, blueberries, and lemon wheels as garnish before serving.

82. CHERRY-LIME RICKEY

Prep Time: 20 Mins

Cook Time: 40 Mins

Total Time: 1 Hr

Servings: 6-8

INGREDIENTS

- 2 cups of pitted fresh or frozen cherries, plus pitted frozen cherries, for serving
- 1 cup of sugar
- ¾ cup of frozen limeade concentrate (half of a 12-ounce can)
- ½ cup of fresh lime juice, plus lime wheels, for serving
- Seltzer for serving (optional)

INSTRUCTIONS

➤ In a medium saucepan over high heat, combine the cherries, sugar, and 1 cup of water. Simmer after coming to a boil. Crush the cherries gently with a potato masher, then boil the mixture for 10 minutes, or until it has slightly reduced and turned dark red. Allow 10 minutes for cooling.

➤ Press down on the cherry solids to extract all the juice while you pour the mixture through a sieve into a heatproof container. There should be roughly 1 ¾ cups of syrup. Allow 30 minutes for cooling.

➤ Mix the limeade, lime juice, and cherry syrup well in a pitcher. There will be approximately 3 cups total.

➤ To serve, stir 3 cups of water into the drink mix for a still beverage, or combine the drink mix and seltzer in equal parts in a glass. Serve with frozen cherries and lime wheels on top of the ice.

83. GOOD MORNING SUNBURST

Total Time: 1 Mins

Servings: 1

INGREDIENTS

- 8 ounces of sparkling water
- 2 tbsp of grenadine syrup (use more or less depending on your preference)
- ½ cup of orange juice frozen into ice cube spheres
- 2 tsp of vanilla syrup (optional) (use more or less depending on your preference)
- 1 sprig of rosemary

INSTRUCTIONS

➢ Place two spheres of orange juice ice cubes in a 12-ounce glass.
➢ Add in sparkling water. Add the grenadine syrup slowly. Pour the vanilla syrup in gradually, if you prefer.
➢ Serve with a straw and a rosemary sprig.

NOTES

1. You may also prepare this recipe with orange juice frozen into regular ice cubes. Use roughly 4-6 ice cubes per drink, depending on the size of your ice cube tray.
2. This genuine grenadine syrup has no corn syrup or artificial colors. Water, Demerara Sugar, Ginger, Cassia Cinnamon, Allspice, Kola Nuts, Anise Seed, and Vanilla Bean are the only ingredients.

84. COPYCAT ICED GUAVA PASSION FRUIT DRINK

Prep Time: 5 Mins

Cook Time: 10 Mins

Total Time: 15 Mins

Servings: 2

INGREDIENTS

For the syrup

- 2 cups of small pineapple chunks, plus two wedges and two pineapple leaves, optional, for garnish
- ⅓ cup of sugar
- 1-inch of fresh ginger, sliced into very thin coins

For each drink

- ¾ cup of unsweetened coconut milk
- ½ cup of guava juice
- 2 tbsp passion fruit juice
- 1 to 2 tbsp pomegranate or tart cherry juice
- Ice

INSTRUCTIONS

- ➢ Combine the pineapple, ½ cup of water, sugar, and ginger in a small saucepan over medium heat. Bring it to a boil. Reduce to a simmer and leave for 10 minutes. Remove from heat and set aside to cool. In a measuring cup or dish, push down on the solids to extract any additional juices, and then strain through a fine-mesh sieve; discard solids.
- ➢ Coconut milk, 1 tbsp each of guava, passionfruit, and pomegranate juices, 2 tsp of pineapple-ginger syrup, and an ice-filled cocktail shaker. If you want a deeper hue, add additional pomegranate juice. Shake vehemently until thoroughly cooled.
- ➢ Pour into two ice-filled glasses. Add a pineapple slice and leaf as garnish.

85. MOCK APPLE-CIDER SOUR

Prep Time: 5 Mins

Servings: 1

INGREDIENTS

- 1 small sugar cube
- 1 tsp freshly squeezed lemon juice
- 2 ounces apple cider
- 2 ounces of cranberry-raspberry flavored seltzer
- 1 spherical piece of cocktail ice
- 1 whole apple chip
- One 2-to 3-inch piece of orange peel

INSTRUCTIONS

➢ In a 6- to 8-ounce Old Fashions glass, mix the seltzer, apple cider, lemon juice, and sugar cube. To dissolve the sugar, stir. Add the apple chip and ice cube sphere. Flame the orange peel by simultaneously bending it with the skin-side out and igniting the orange oil spraying from the peel with a match or lighter. Before adding the peel to the beverage, rub it over the rim of the glass.

86. HOLIDAY CRANBERRY MOJITO RECIPE

Prep Time: 15 Mins

Cook Time: 15 Mins

Total Time: 30 Mins

Servings: 4

INGREDIENTS

For the Cranberry Simple Syrup

- 225g of fresh cranberries
- 1 Cup of Sugar
- 1 Cup of Water

For the Holiday Cranberry Mojito Recipe

- 120 ml Orange Juice
- 120 ml Simple Syrup
- 120 ml of store-bought limeade or soda water
- Ice cubes as needed
- 30 Mint leaves
- 8 Lemon slices or Lime slices

Garnishes

- Mint leaves
- Fresh cranberries

INSTRUCTIONS

➢ Cranberries, sugar, and water are combined in a medium pot and simmered.
➢ When the berries start to burst after 5 minutes, put the lid on the pan. Stop the heat and let them cool.
➢ Mix them in a blender until smooth, then strain to get the simple cranberry syrup.
➢ Prepare glasses for serving. With a muddler, mash in some mint leaves and lemon slices.
➢ Pour 30 ml of cranberry syrup followed by enough ice cubes into each glass.
➢ Add the necessary amount of limeade or sparkling water on top of the 30ml of orange juice.
➢ Add the desired amount of limeade or sparkling water on top.
➢ Cranberries and mint leaves make a nice garnish.

87. EGGNOG ORANGE JULIUS

Total Time: 5 Mins

Servings: 6

INGREDIENTS

- One 6 ounce can of frozen orange juice concentrate
- 1 cup of eggnog
- 1 cup of water
- 1 tsp vanilla
- ⅓ cup of sugar
- 2 cups of ice cubes
- ¼ tsp ground nutmeg, optional

Garnish
- whipped cream
- dash ground nutmeg

INSTRUCTIONS

➤ Add all of the ingredients to the blender with the eggnog and water. For two minutes, blend on high speed.
➤ Pour into glasses.
➤ Serve with whipped cream and nutmeg.

88. LIME ZINGER

Total Time: 5 Mins

Servings: 1

INGREDIENTS

- 2 cucumber strips
- 3-lime wheels
- ice
- Red Bull Lime Edition Sugar free
- white grape juice
- Speared strawberry halves

INSTRUCTIONS

➤ Add ice, lime wheels, and cucumber to a glass. Red Bull Lime Edition Sugar free in a ratio of 8 ounces to 2 ounces of white grape juice, or 4 parts Red Bull Lime Edition Sugar free to 1 part white grape juice. Serve with speared strawberry halves as a garnish.

89. HONEY ORANGEADE

Prep Time: 15 Mins

Cook Time: 1 Hr

Total: 1 Hr 15 Mins

Servings: 4

INGREDIENTS

- Orange Honey Syrup
- 24 ounces of chilled seltzer
- For garnish, orange slices

Orange Honey Syrup:

- ½ cup of honey
- 1 cup of fresh-squeezed orange juice plus 4 strips of orange peel (no white pith)

INSTRUCTIONS

➤ Add ice to four 12-ounce glasses. Divide the orange honey syrup among the glasses, then add the seltzer on top. Combine, stir, and top with orange slices.

Orange Honey Syrup

➤ In a small saucepan over medium heat, stir the orange juice, orange peel, and honey until the mixture is hot and the honey has dissolved. Remove from the heat and allow the food to cool to room temperature.

90. COPYCAT STARBUCKS CARAMEL FRAPPUCCINO

Total Time: 10 Mins

Servings: 2

INGREDIENTS

- 1 cup of cold, strong-brewed coffee
- ¾ cup of whole milk
- ½ cup of caramel, plus more for serving
- 1 cup of ice
- whipped cream for serving

INSTRUCTIONS

➤ Blend milk, coffee, vanilla, and 1 cup of ice until smooth, thick, and Icey. If more ice is needed to get the correct consistency, do so.
➤ Pour into glasses, then add whipped cream over top. Add more caramel sauce.

91. MOCK MULE

Prep Time: 5 Mins

Servings: 1

INGREDIENTS

- 6 ounces of ginger beer
- 3 ounces lime-flavor seltzer
- 1 large piece of candied ginger, roughly chopped
- Lime wedge, for garnish

INSTRUCTIONS

➢ Crush ice into a 16-ounce copper mug. Add the seltzer and ginger beer. Add a lime wedge and candied ginger as garnish.

92. RASPBERRY FIZZLER

Prep Time: 5 Mins

Servings: 2

INGREDIENTS

- 1 ½ cups of raspberry juice
- 3 scoops of raspberry sherbet
- ½ cup of carbonated water

INSTRUCTIONS

➢ Blend raspberry juice, raspberry sherbet, and carbonated water in a blender. Blend until smooth. Pour into serving glasses.

93. TART APPLE-GINGER SHRUB

Prep Time: 10 Mins

Total Time: 4 Days 10 Mins

Servings: 8

INGREDIENTS

- 1 shredded Granny Smith apple
- ⅓ cup of unfiltered apple cider vinegar
- ¼ cup of white sugar
- 1 tsp grated fresh ginger

INSTRUCTIONS

➤ Place the apple in a glass jar with a tight-fitting cover. Stir in the apple cider vinegar, sugar, and ginger. Close tightly. Allow 4 to 5 days in the refrigerator.
➤ Strain the syrupy liquid into a clean container, discarding the apple scraps. Close tightly and chill.

94. GINGER GASTRIQUE

Total Time: 20 Mins

Servings: 1

INGREDIENTS

- ½ cup of minced fresh ginger
- 4 ounces of apple cider vinegar
- 2 ounces of sherry vinegar
- 2 ounces of water
- 1 cup of sugar

INSTRUCTIONS

➤ In a small skillet, bring the ingredients to a simmer. Add the sugar, stir, and then boil for 20 minutes. In a heatproof jar, fine-strain. Let it cool and store in the fridge for up to 2 weeks.

95. THANKSGIVING MOCKTAIL

Prep Time: 15 Mins

Total Time: 1 Hr

Servings: 2

INGREDIENTS

- ½ cup of blood orange juice plus 2 blood orange slices for serving
- ⅓ cup of sugar
- 4 large sprigs of fresh thyme
- 1 ¼ cups of non-alcoholic ginger beer
- ½ cup of cranberry juice
- Frozen cranberries for serving

INSTRUCTIONS

➢ Heat the blood orange juice, sugar, and thyme in a small saucepan over medium heat. Mixing to dissolve sugar, bring to a simmer while stirring, and cook for 2 minutes to allow the flavors to meld. Turn off the heat and let the mixture steep and cool to room temperature.

➢ Remove the thyme and drain the syrup through a strainer. The syrup may now be covered and stored in the refrigerator for up to a week or until it is time to use it.

➢ To 2 highball glasses with ice, add 2 tsp of the blood-orange syrup. Add half of the ginger beer and half of the cranberry juice to each glass's rim. Stir, then garnish with a slice of blood orange and some frozen cranberries.

96. MOCK CHAMPAGNE

Prep Time: 1 Day 15 Mins

Servings: 40

INGREDIENTS

- 2-liter chilled ginger ale
- 46 fluid ounces of chilled pineapple juice
- 64 fluid ounces of chilled white grape juice

INSTRUCTIONS

- ➤ To make ice ring: Ginger ale is poured halfway into a ring-shaped cake pan. Freeze until frozen partially. At this stage, you can put edible flowers or pieces of fruit around the ring. Fill the pan with ginger ale, then freeze it until firm. Place in a punch bowl just before serving.
- ➤ Mix 1 bottle of ginger ale, pineapple juice, and white grape juice in a big punch bowl.

97. STRAWBERRY LEMONADE

Prep Time: 5 Mins

Cook Time: 20 Mins

Total Time: 25 Mins

Servings: 6

INGREDIENTS

- 1 cup of granulated sugar
- 6 cups of divided water
- 1 pound of hulled and halved strawberries
- 1 cup of freshly squeezed lemon juice
- Ice
- Mint leaves (optional)

INSTRUCTIONS

- ➤ Mix sugar and 1 cup of water over medium heat in a small saucepan. Bring it to a boil and simmer until dissolved. Let cool.
- ➤ Mix strawberries and 1 cup of water in a blender. Blend until smooth. Drain the puree and remove any remaining solids using a sieve with a fine mesh.
- ➤ Combine simple syrup, strawberry puree, lemon juice, and the remaining 4 cups of water in a large pitcher. Adjust to taste with more water or lemon juice.
- ➤ If preferred, serve with mint over ice.

98. GRAPEFRUIT-COCONUT COOLER

Prep Time: 5 Mins

Servings: 1

INGREDIENTS

- 2 ounces of cream of coconut
- 8 ounces of Ruby Red grapefruit juice or pink grapefruit juice
- ½ ounce of agave nectar

INSTRUCTIONS

- ➤ Stir together the grapefruit juice, coconut cream, and agave in a small pitcher or bowl. Pour into a glass over ice.

99. ITALIAN CREAM SODA

Prep Time: 1 Mins

Servings: 1

INGREDIENTS

- 8 fluid ounces of carbonated water
- ¾ fluid ounce passion fruit flavored syrup
- ¾ fluid ounces of watermelon-flavored syrup
- 1 fluid ounce of half-and-half cream

INSTRUCTIONS

➤ Fill a large glass halfway with ice. Fill up to ⅔ with carbonated water. Pour in the watermelon and passion fruit syrups, then top with the half-and-half cream. Mix well just before serving.

100. THAI ICED TEA

Total Time: 30 Mins

Servings: 4

INGREDIENTS

- 4 cups of water
- ½ cup of Thai tea mix
- ½ cup of granulated sugar
- Ice
- Sweetened condensed milk

INSTRUCTIONS

➤ Bring the water to a boil. Mix boiling water, Thai tea, and sugar in a big pitcher. Allow it to steep for 15 minutes.
➤ Remove all of the liquid from the tea leaves using a strainer with a fine mesh. Chill for at least 2 hours, or until completely cold.
➤ When ready to serve, pour tea over ice and top each glass with 2 tbsp of sweetened condensed milk.

101. VIRGIN MANGO MARGARITAS

Prep Time: 5 Mins

Servings: 8

INGREDIENTS

- Two 20-ounce jars of mango chunks, drained
- Ice, for blending
- One 250-milliliter bottle of lemon-lime soda
- 2 tbsp of sugar

INSTRUCTIONS

➤ Blend the mango chunks in a blender. Fill the blender with ice. Pour in the soda and sugar and mix until fully smooth, adding more ice as needed to get the desired consistency. Pour the beverages and serve them right away.

102. TORNADO TWIST

Total Time: 1 Mins

Servings: 2

INGREDIENTS

- 12 fluid ounces of cranberry-raspberry juice
- 12 fluid ounce or bottle of lemon-lime flavored carbonated beverage

INSTRUCTIONS

➤ Combine cranberry-raspberry juice and lemon-lime soda in a pitcher. Pour over ice and enjoy.

103. MEADOW MOCKTAILS

Total Time: 20 Mins

Servings: 8

INGREDIENTS

Lavender syrup

- 1 cup of sugar
- 1 cup of water
- ¼ cup of dried lavender flowers

Mocktails

- ½ cup of basil leaves
- 2 tbsp of fresh lemon juice
- 11 ounces of chilled fresh grapefruit juice
- ¼ ounces Angostura bitters
- 40 ounces of chilled sparkling water
- Ice
- For garnish: basil leaves, grapefruit slices or lavender flowers

INSTRUCTIONS

- ➢ Prepare the lavender syrup.
- ➢ In a medium saucepan, bring all of the ingredients to a boil. Cook over moderate heat, stirring, until the sugar dissolves, about 3 minutes. Remove it from the heat, cover, and set aside for 2 hours to steep. Using a fine sieve, strain the syrup.
- ➢ Prepare the mocktails.
- ➢ Pulse the basil and lemon juice in a small food processor until chopped. Pour into a big pitcher. 11 ounces of lavender syrup (any remaining syrup may be kept for 2 weeks), grapefruit juice, bitters, and sparkling water. Pour into ice-filled glasses and top with basil.

104. CRANBERRY SPRITZER

Total Time: 8 Mins

Servings: 4

INGREDIENTS

- 12 ice cubes
- 2 ½ cups of seltzer
- 2 cups of cranberry juice
- 2 tbsp of honey
- 1 thinly sliced orange

INSTRUCTIONS

➢ Put ice cubes in the pitcher. Add seltzer. To a big pitcher, add 2 cups of cranberry juice. Add in 2 tbsp of honey. Add the orange slices and stir to combine.

105. STRAWBERRY-MINT SODA

Prep Time: 10 Mins

Servings: 8

INGREDIENTS

➢ 2 large quartered limes
➢ ½ bunch of mint leaves
➢ 7 quartered strawberries
➢ 1 cup of white sugar
➢ 3 cups of carbonated water

INSTRUCTIONS

➢ Squeeze the lime quarters into a strong glass pitcher. Combine the mint, strawberries, sugar, and juiced limes in a pitcher. Mix the fruits together to release the juices from the strawberries and the oil from the mint leaves. When Club soda is added; stir until sugar is dissolved. Pour the ice cubes into the sugared glasses to serve.

106. CHICHA MORADA

Prep Time: 30 Mins

Cook Time: 4 Hrs 30 Mins

Total Time: 5 Hrs

Servings: 9

INGREDIENTS

- 1 pineapple (3 /2-pound trimmed, peeled and cored, peel and core reserved, one-quarter of the pineapple diced)
- 2 Granny Smith apples
- 1 bag of dried purple corn
- 2 cinnamon sticks
- ½ tsp whole cloves
- ¾ cup of light brown sugar
- ½ cup of fresh lemon juice (plus 2 tbsp of fresh lemon juice)
- ½ cup of fresh lime juice (plus 2 tbsp of fresh lime juice)
- 1 tsp kosher salt
- Ice (for serving)
- Lime wheels (for garnish)

INSTRUCTIONS

➤ Add the pineapple peel and core, quartered apple, purple corn, cinnamon sticks, cloves, sugar, and 14 cups of water to a large saucepan. Over moderately high heat, cover and bring to a boil. Turn down the heat, remove the lid, and simmer for about an hour, or until the corn is softened and the liquid has slightly decreased.

➤ Remove and discard the solids using a slotted spoon. Pour the liquid into a large heatproof bowl through a fine-mesh strainer, and then let it there for 45 minutes, or until it stops steaming. Once the chicha morada is very cold, for about 2 hours, mix in the salt, lime juice, and lemon juice.

➤ The remaining apple is peeled, cored, and sliced neatly. In a pitcher, combine the apple and cubed pineapple. Then, add the chicha morada. Serve in glasses with ice and lime wheels for garnish.

107. WINTER SPICE LEMONADE

Prep Time: 10 Mins

Cook Time: 15 Mins

Total Time: 25 Mins

Servings: 8

INGREDIENTS

- 1 ½ cups of sugar
- 3 cinnamon sticks
- 3 star anise pods
- One 3-inch peeled and sliced piece of fresh ginger
- 6 cups of chilled seltzer
- 1 ½ cups of lemon juice

INSTRUCTIONS

- ➤ In a small saucepan, combine 1 ½ cups of water, ginger, sugar, cinnamon sticks, and star anise pods. Bring it to a boil, then remove it from the heat and allow to cool to room temperature. strain.
- ➤ Mix the filtered simple syrup, cool seltzer, and lemon juice in a big pitcher. Stir and pour into ice-filled glasses.

108. RASPBERRY LIME RICKEY

Total Time: 2 Mins

Servings: 1

INGREDIENTS

- 1 quarter lime
- 8 fluid ounces of carbonated water
- 1.5 fluid ounce jigger raspberry syrup

INSTRUCTIONS

➤ Add ice to a large glass. Drop each slice of lime into the glass once it has been squeezed. Add raspberry syrup to the top of the almost full glass of carbonated water.

109. CUCUMBER-LEMONADE MOCKTAIL

Total Time: 10 Mins

Servings: 1

INGREDIENTS

- 1 paper-thin, lengthwise dice of European cucumber for garnish
- Ice
- 1 tbsp agave syrup
- ¼ tsp finely sliced dill, plus 1 dill sprig, for garnish
- ¼ cup of chilled club soda
- 1 tbsp fresh lime juice
- 1 tbsp fresh lemon juice
- ¼ cup of fresh cucumber juice

INSTRUCTIONS

➤ Add ice to a chilled highball glass, then press a cucumber slice against the inside of the glass. Mix the chopped dill, agave syrup, lime and lemon juices, and 1 tbsp of water in a cocktail shaker until the syrup is dissolved. Add ice, then add the cucumber juice and vigorously shake in a prepared glass—strain and top with club soda. Add the dill sprig as a garnish.

NOTES

1. You can also use a mixer to puree chunks of peeled cucumber, then strain the puree through a fine sieve. About ¾ cup of juice can be strained from one large cucumber.

110. ORANGE CREAM MIMOSA

Total Time: 4 Hr 10 Mins

Servings: 8-10

INGREDIENTS

- 2 ½ cups of orange juice, freshly squeezed
- 1 zested orange
- 1 cup of half-and-half
- 1 cup of superfine sugar
- 1 bottle of alcohol-free sparkling wine
- Strawberries, for garnish
- Ginger ale, sparkling cider, or non-alcoholic sparkling wine may be used in its place.

INSTRUCTIONS

- ➢ Blend the orange juice, zest, half-and-half, and sugar for approximately 30 seconds, or until the sugar has completely dissolved. Pour this mixture into a pan and freeze for four hours or more until solid.
- ➢ Take the frozen orange mixture out of the freezer and let it out for 10 minutes to slightly soften. Scrape out a small scoop and place it in a champagne glass using a scoop or tbsp. Fill the glass slowly with alcohol-free Sparkling wine and garnish with strawberries.

111. BLUEBERRY-GINGER FIZZ

Prep Time: 10 Mins

Cook Time: 10 Mins

Additional: 10 Mins

Total Time: 30 Mins

Servings: 1

INGREDIENTS

Blueberry-Ginger Syrup

- 1-pint blueberries
- 1 cup of water
- ¼ cup of sugar
- 1 tbsp grated fresh ginger
- ¼ cup of crushed ice
- 2 tbsp of orange juice
- ¼ cup of club soda
- 1 slice orange (Optional)

INSTRUCTIONS

➤ In a pan over medium-high heat, bring the blueberries, water, sugar, and ginger to a boil. Cook for 5 minutes with the heat reduced to a simmer, occasionally crushing the blueberries with a fork. After about 10 minutes, remove it from the heat and allow it to cool. To get the blueberries' skins out of the mixture, run it through a food mill or fine mesh sieve. Set aside ¼ cup of the syrup and keep the rest in the refrigerator for up to a week.

➤ Place crushed ice in a glass. Add the reserved blueberry-ginger syrup and orange juice. Add club soda to the top and stir to combine. An orange slice as a garnish

112. ALMOND-FENNEL COOLER

Total Time: 35 Mins

Servings: 1

INGREDIENTS

- ¾ ounce of orgeat (almond-flavored syrup)
- ¾ ounce Fennel Syrup
- ½ ounce of fresh lemon juice
- Ice
- 6 ounces of chilled club soda
- 1 fennel frond for garnish (optional)

INSTRUCTIONS

➤ Mix thoroughly with the orgeat, fennel syrup, and fresh lemon juice in a Collins glass. Pour in the ice, then the cooled club soda, and garnish with the fennel frond.

113. WASSAIL

Total Time: 1 Hr

Servings: 6-8

INGREDIENTS

- One 4-inch piece of fresh peeled ginger, thinly sliced
- 2 tsp whole allspice berries
- 2 tsp whole cloves
- ½ gallon of apple cider
- 2 cups of cranberry juice
- 1 cup of pineapple juice
- 1 medium orange, thinly sliced into rounds, plus more for garnish
- 2 tbsp of maple syrup, plus more to taste

INSTRUCTIONS

➤ Tie the ginger, allspice, and cloves in a 10-inch square of cheesecloth. Bring the spice bundle, apple cider, cranberry juice, pineapple juice, and orange slices to a simmer in a large saucepan over medium heat. Simmer for 35 to 40 minutes, or until the wassail is aromatic. Remove the spice bundle and orange slices using a slotted spoon. Mix in the 2 tbsp of maple syrup, then add more to taste. Serve it garnished with more orange slices.

114. BROOD BREW

Total Time: 5 Mins

Servings: 4- 6

INGREDIENTS

- 5 ounces of fresh apple cider
- 5 ounces of maple syrup
- 3 ounces of pear puree or juice
- 2 ounces of fresh lemon juice
- 1 heaping tsp of ground cinnamon
- 5 ounces of sparkling clear non-alcoholic cider

INSTRUCTIONS

➤ Special equipment: Punch bowls and bizarre straws are optional.
➤ In a large cocktail shaker, combine the apple cider, maple syrup, pear puree, lemon juice, and cinnamon and dry-shake until the cinnamon is well mixed. Put the mixture in a small punch bowl with a big chunk of ice and mix it around until it's cool.
➤ Pour into mason jars, top with sparkling non-alcoholic cider, and serve with a crazy straw.

NOTES

1. Chill water in a plastic or metal bowl slightly smaller than the punch bowl to form a huge ice cube.

115. THE ARNOLD PALMER

Total time: 5 mins

Servings: 1

INGREDIENTS

- 5 fluid ounces of prepared lemonade
- 5 fluid ounces of prepared iced tea
- 1 cup of ice

INSTRUCTIONS

➢ In a highball or large glass, mix lemonade and iced tea. Stir in ice and continue until cooled.

116. FRUIT INFUSED SPARKLING MOCKTAILS

Total Time: 4 Hrs 15 Mins

Servings: 3

INGREDIENTS

- Fruit-infused ice cubes
- Raspberries
- blackberries
- Cranberries, dried or fresh
- Mint leaves
- water
- Sparkling Berry Pomegranate
- sparkling water
- pomegranate juice
- Fresh blackberries and raspberries
- Fruit-infused ice cubes
- Sparkling Orange

- sparkling water
- orange juice
- Orange slices
- Fruit-infused ice cubes
- Sparkling Watermelon Mint
- sparkling water
- Mint leaves
- watermelon chunks
- Fruit-infused ice cubes

INSTRUCTIONS

- ➢ Fruit-infused ice cubes
- ➢ Distribute the fruits and mint leaves in an ice cube tray. Add water on top, then freeze for at least four hours.

117. MOCK MANGO FIZZ

Total Time: 5 Mins

Servings: 1

INGREDIENTS

- ¼ cup of orange juice
- 2 tbsp of grapefruit juice
- ⅔ cup of mango-flavored seltzer
- Orange twist, for garnish

INSTRUCTIONS

- ➢ Add the orange and grapefruit juices in a 10- to 14-ounce Tom Collins glass. Fill the glass with crushed ice. Top off with the seltzer. Add an orange twist as a garnish.

118. ALCOHOL-FREE MOJITOS

Total Time: 15 Mins

Servings: 14

INGREDIENTS

- 2 cups of water
- 1 ½ cups of white sugar
- 2 cups of chopped mint leaves
- 2 cups of softened lime sherbet
- 1 cup of lime juice
- 1 cup of water
- 8 cups of club soda
- Lime slices for garnish

INSTRUCTIONS

➤ In a microwave-safe bowl, mix 2 cups of water and the sugar. Microwave on high for 5 minutes. Water and mint are combined, then let to stand for 5 minutes. Remove the syrup from the mint leaves and discard them.

➤ In a large pitcher, thoroughly mix the lime sherbet, lime juice, and 1 cup of water. Pour the syrup with the mint into the mixture. Stir in the club soda. Serve chilled. slices of lime as a garnish.

119. STRAWBERRY MOJITO MOCKTAIL

Total Time: 3 Mins

Servings: 1

INGREDIENTS

- 3 hulled and quartered strawberries
- 16 mint leaves
- 1 lime
- 1 lime-flavored seltzer

INSTRUCTIONS

➢ In a glass, combine the strawberries and mint using a fork. Pour the lime juice into the glass. Add ice to the glass. Over the top, pour the seltzer. Garnish with more strawberries, mint, and lime slices.

NOTES

1. For garnishing, use more of everything on the ingredient list above. For example, additional strawberries, a few leaves, and a few lime slices on top are a nice touch.

120. CHRISTMAS MOCKTAILS

Total Time: 5 Mins

Servings: 6

INGREDIENTS

- 4 cups of cranberry juice
- 2 cups of pineapple juice
- 2 cups of orange juice
- ice
- sprite or sparkling water (optional)
- sugar for glass rims

INSTRUCTIONS

➢ In a pitcher, combine the cranberry, orange, and pineapple juices. Sprite and ice are added (or sparkling water).
➢ If desired, dip the wet edges of the glasses into sugar.
➢ Serve after pouring into glasses.

121. MEXICAN STRAWBERRY WATER

Total Time: 4 Hrs 25 Mins

Servings: 10

INGREDIENTS

- 4 cups of sliced strawberries
- 1 cup of white sugar
- 8 cups of cold water
- 1 lime, cut into 8 wedges
- 8 fresh mint sprigs

INSTRUCTIONS

➤ Combine the cut strawberries, sugar, and 1 cup of water in a medium mixing bowl. In the refrigerator for 4 hours, wrap plastic wrap around the bowl.

➤ Take the strawberry mixture from the refrigerator and place it in a blender. Blend until smooth, on high. Put a wire mesh strainer over a large mixing bowl, and pour the blended berry mixture through it. Discard the pulp and seeds.

➤ Mix the pureed strawberries with the remaining 7 cups of cold water. Refrigerate the Aqua de Fresa for several hours, or serve immediately over ice. Add lime slices or mint leaves as garnish.

122. PINA COLADA MOCKTAIL

Total Time: 15 Mins

Servings: 4

INGREDIENTS

- 2 cups of chilled pineapple juice
- ½ cup of chilled cream of coconut
- ¼ cup of chilled coconut cream
- 3-4 cups of ice

INSTRUCTIONS

➤ Blend all ingredients together in a blender with 3 glasses of ice until completely smooth.

➤ Add additional ice and blend again until desired consistency.

NOTES

1. By the wine and beer, on the aisle with the mix-ins, is a squeeze bottle of cream of coconut.

2. Canned cream of coconut is found in the ethnic food isles.

123. BLUEBERRY MOCKTAIL WITH MINT AND LIME

Total Time: 5 Mins

Servings: 1

INGREDIENTS

- ½ ounce lime juice
- 1-2 tbsp of frozen pink lemonade concentrate
- 2 tbsp frozen blueberries
- 6-8 leaves of fresh mint
- 2 ounces of coconut water
- 3 ounces of club soda (or soda of choice)
- ice cubes

INSTRUCTIONS

➤ In a glass, combine lime juice, frozen pink lemonade concentrate, frozen blueberries, and fresh mint leaves.

➤ 1 to 2 tbsp of frozen pink lemonade concentrate, 1/2 an ounce of lime juice, and 6 to 8 fresh mint leaves

➤ Gently mix blueberries and mint leaves by softly pushing down on the mint leaves to release their flavor. Try not to rip the mint leaves.

➤ Serve the drink with a few ice cubes before adding the coconut water.

➤ ice cubes and 2 ounces of coconut water

➤ Add club soda on top (or soda of choice).

➤ 3 ounces. Club soda

➤ garnish is optional.

➤ Serve right away and enjoy!

124. HABANERO LEMONADE

Prep Time: 10 Mins

Cook Time: 1 Hr 30 Mins

Total Time: 1 Hr 40 Mins

Servings: 16

INGREDIENTS

- 1-gallon water
- 12 lemons
- 3 habanero peppers seeds were removed and sliced
- 3 cups of sugar
- Lemon slices for serving, optional

INSTRUCTIONS

➢ Slice the lemons in half, then press the juice into a bowl. Place the bowl aside.
➢ Add the sugar to a pot with 2 cups of water. Once the saucepan has reached a rolling boil, reduce the heat to a simmer.
➢ Add the habanero peppers to the sugar water and continue to cook for 10 minutes, stirring regularly.
➢ After turning off the heat, take the pot and the slices of habanero from the water.
➢ Add the sugar water, lemon juice, and remaining water to a big pitcher. Good stirring
➢ Put the pitcher in the fridge and, at the very least, give the lemonade 30-60 minutes to chill.
➢ Serve chilled. Add lemon slices as desired.

125. GUMMY BEAR MOCKTAIL

Total Time: 25 Mins

Servings: 8

INGREDIENTS

- 8 plastic stemless champagne flutes
- 8 plastic swizzle sticks
- 8 fun paper straws
- 1 toothpick
- Two 25.4-ounce bottles of sparkling apple cider
- 10 ounces of gummy bears
- ¼ Cup of granulated sugar
- a shallow dish with water

INSTRUCTIONS

- ➢ Insert one of each color of a gummy bear onto each of 8 plastic swizzle sticks. First, use a toothpick to poke the gummy bears all the way through, one at a time. This will make inserting the swizzle stick into each bear simpler.
- ➢ Sugar the rim of every champagne flute. Dip the rim of each flute one at a time into a shallow dish of water and then into a shallow dish of granulated sugar. Place a small handful of gummy bears at the bottom of each wine glass. Consider using one of each color if your party guests are young children (i.e., less sugar in hyper kids).
- ➢ Pour each flute with sparkling apple cider until it is three-quarters full. Use the gummy bear swizzle sticks as garnish. Finally, decorate each flute with a colorful party straw. Serve right away.

NOTES

1. Many gummy bears include gelatin. Bunny Fruit Snacks and Surf Sweet Organic Fruity Bears will suffice to make this recipe vegetarian and vegan. Consider using sparkling apple cider and organic gummy bears to make this recipe less processed and healthy.

126. LEMON BASIL SPRITZER

Total Time: 1 Mins

Servings: 1

INGREDIENTS

Skip the first two ingredients if using Stevia instead of simple syrup.

- ½ cup of water
- ½ cup of granulated sugar

Spritzer recipe:
- 3 leaves of fresh basil
- 2 lemon slices
- ¾ cup of cold sparkling water
- 2 tbsp of simple syrup
- 2 tbsp of freshly squeezed lemon juice
- Basil leaves or lemon wedges for garnish

INSTRUCTIONS

- ➢ If using simple syrup, bring water and sugar to a boil in a pot, then reduce to a low heat and simmer for 6 minutes. Allow it to cool completely. If using liquid stevia, skip this step.
- ➢ To make drink, muddle a few basil leaves and two lemon wedges in the bottom of the glass, crushing the lemon slices and basil together.
- ➢ Muddle in the lemon juice and either simple syrup or stevia drops. Then, into the glass, add the tonic water.
- ➢ If preferred, add a few ice cubes and garnish with more basil and lemon wedges.

127. MEXICAN MULE MOCKTAIL

Prep Time: 5 Mins

Serving: 1

INGREDIENTS

- 50ml Non-Alcoholic Tequila
- Ginger Beer
- 25ml Fresh Lime Juice
- 2 x Small Pieces of Ginger
- Lime - To Garnish

INSTRUCTIONS

- ➢ Pour mixture into copper mug once muddled ginger and additional ingredients are combined in a shaker.
- ➢ Ginger beer and ice go here.
- ➢ Adding a lime wedge as garnish.

128. CRANBERRY LIMEADE SPARKLING MOCKTAIL RECIPE

Total Time: 5 Mins

Servings: 16

INGREDIENTS

- 5 ounces of frozen limeade concentrate
- 64 ounces of cranberry juice
- 2 liters of Sprite
- Fresh cranberries
- Lime slices

INSTRUCTIONS

- ➢ Add limeade concentrate to a large glass pitcher. Pour in cranberry juice and stir the mixture quickly to break up the frozen limeade concentrate. Pour the soda in slowly and mix it again. Serve with lime wedges and fresh cranberries as garnish!

129. EASY CITRUS STRAWBERRY MOCKTAIL RECIPE

Prep Time: 5 Mins

Cook Time: 10 Mins

Total Time: 15 Mins

INGREDIENTS

For the Strawberry Simple Syrup

- 1 cup of water
- 1 cup of sugar
- 1 cup of chopped strawberries, pulsed in a blender

For the Mocktail

- 1 TBS strawberry simple syrup
- 1 cup of lemon-lime soda
- 1 tsp lime juice
- 1 TBS macerated strawberries optional

INSTRUCTIONS

For the Simple Syrup

- In a pot, combine strawberries, sugar, and water.
- Heat over medium heat until boiling.
- Mix while boiling until the sugar is completely dissolved.
- Pour the mixture through a fine-mesh strainer to remove any remaining strawberry syrup. If you want to add more flavor to the citrus strawberry mocktail, toss in some of the remaining strawberry mixture.

For the mocktail

- Combine simple strawberry syrup, lemon-lime soda, lime juice, and macerated strawberries for the ultimate citrus mocktail!

NOTES

1. Multiple drinks may be made using the simple syrup recipe.
2. Use more macerated strawberries from the simple strawberry syrup to make your beverage sweeter.
3. Use half (or none) of the macerated strawberries and club soda in favor of the lemon-lime soda if you like a less sweet beverage.

130. SUNSET MICHELADA

Total Time: 5 Mins

Servings: 1

INGREDIENTS

Vegetable Juice

- 2 pints of sweet cherry tomatoes
- ¼ cup of chopped celery
- ¼ cup of chopped red bell pepper
- salt and ground black pepper to taste

Michelada

- ½ tsp flake sea salt
- 1 pinch of freshly ground black pepper
- 1 pinch of dried red chile pepper
- 1 halved lime
- ice cubes
- ½ tsp Worcestershire sauce
- ½ tsp hot pepper sauce
- ⅛ tsp soy sauce
- ¼ cup of homemade vegetable juice
- 12 fluid ounces of ice-cold Mexican lager

INSTRUCTIONS

> ➢ Blend the celery, red bell pepper, and cherry tomatoes. Pulse a few times to get the mixture moving. Blend on high for a few more seconds or until the mixture has liquefied. Strain the mixture over a bowl to remove seeds and skins. To extract the liquid, use a spatula to push the mixture through the strainer—season with salt and pepper.
>
> ➢ On a small plate, sprinkle chili pepper, black pepper, and salt flakes. Use the sliced surface of lime to rub the glass rim. Invert the glass and dip the edge into the salt mixture.
>
> ➢ Pour Worcestershire sauce, spicy sauce, and soy sauce into a glass filled with ice. Pour in the veggie juice and ½ lime juice. ¾ fill the glass with an ice-cold beer. Stir. Add additional beer. Slice of lime as a garnish.

NOTES

1. Cover vegetable juice with plastic wrap and chill if not drinking immediately. If it settles, it may need stirring.

131. GINGER MOJITO MOCKTAIL NONALCOHOLIC

Total Time: 10 Mins

Servings: 1

INGREDIENTS

- 1 inch of grated ginger
- 1 inch of grated cucumber
- Juice of half a lime
- 6 mint leaves
- 0.5 cup of sparkling water
- 0.5 cup of ginger ale

INSTRUCTIONS

> ➢ In a bowl, muddle the ginger, cucumber, and lime.
> ➢ Clap mint leaves together to release the scent, then add to ginger mixture and gently press.
> ➢ Then strain the ingredients into a glass, and fill with ice.

- ➢ Add sparkling water and half the ginger beer to the top.
- ➢ Serve with garnish.

132. MANGO MOJITO MOCKTAIL

Total Time: 10 Mins

Servings: 2

INGREDIENTS

- 2 tbsp of freshly squeezed lime juice
- 2 tbsp of Extra Fine Granulated Sugar
- 10 mint leaves
- 3 tbsp of mango puree (fresh mango, pureed in blender)
- ½ cup of club soda

INSTRUCTIONS

- ➢ Add sugar, lime juice, mint leaves, and mango puree to a big glass or container. Crush mint leaves with the back of a spoon for about a minute to release their smell and taste. Combined with soda.
- ➢ Pour into glasses with ice, and serve.

133. FRESH GRAPEFRUIT MOCKTAIL (NON-ALCOHOLIC)

Cook Time: 10 Mins
Resting Time: 1 Hr
Total Time: 1 Hr 10 Mins
Servings: 4

INGREDIENTS

- 2 grapefruits, juiced, about 1.5 cups of fresh juice
- 4-5 sage leaves
- 12 Ounces unflavored or grapefruit flavored seltzer
- 1 cup of crushed ice
- 3 tbsp lemon zest salt, optional

INSTRUCTIONS

- ➢ Optional: Salt the glass's rim
- ➢ Cut the grapefruit in half and run each half around the rim of four small cups. Dip each glass in a shallow dish of sea salt.
- ➢ Get the drink ready!
- ➢ Remove any seeds before juicing two grapefruits. Simmer the juice in a small saucepan.
- ➢ Stir everything together for around 5 minutes while adding 4-5 sage leaves (or until reduced by about a third).
- ➢ Take out the leaves, then put the juice in the fridge to cool.
- ➢ Give each of the four glasses some juice. Fill each glass with crushed ice until it is 3/4 full.
- ➢ To add a little sparkle, pour some grapefruit-flavored seltzer on top!

134. PINEAPPLE GINGER BEER MOCKTAIL

Total Time: 5 Mins

Servings: 1

INGREDIENTS

- ½ tsp finely chopped ginger
- 3 tbsp mint leaves
- ½-ounce lime juice
- 1 ounce of simple syrup
- 1 ½ ounce of pineapple juice
- 2 ½ ounces of ginger beer

INSTRUCTIONS

- ➢ Combine lime juice, ginger, and mint leaves in a cocktail shaker.
- ➢ Muddle with a muddler.
- ➢ Add pineapple juice and simple syrup.
- ➢ Shake for about 30 seconds with the lid on.
- ➢ Then drain into an ice-filled glass.
- ➢ Add the ginger beer on top and stir. Serve and enjoy!

135. SPARKLING CRANBERRY KOMBUCHA MOCKTAIL

Total Time: 10 Mins

Servings: 4

INGREDIENTS

- 2 bottles of your preferred kombucha (original or unflavored, ginger, cranberry)
- ½ cup of cranberry juice
- 1-inch slice of fresh ginger, thinly sliced, plus more for garnish
- 1 large sprig of fresh rosemary, plus more for garnish
- Fresh cranberries, rosemary sprigs, and thinly sliced ginger for garnish

INSTRUCTIONS

➢ Set aside 4 double old-fashioned glasses filled with ice and place them aside.
➢ Use a wooden spoon end or a muddler, if you have one, to muddle rosemary and ginger slices together in a quart-sized mason jar or pitcher.
➢ Stir in the cranberry juice and kombucha.
➢ Pour into glasses with ice (using a strainer, if required) and top with cranberries, rosemary sprigs, and fresh ginger before serving.

136. POMEGRANATE GINGER SPRITZER

Total time: 10 mins

Servings: 7

INGREDIENTS

- ½ cup of sliced fresh ginger root
- 1 medium sliced lime
- 3 cups of pomegranate juice
- ¾ cup of orange juice
- 3 cups of chilled club soda
- Optional: Lime wedges, pomegranate seeds, and ice

INSTRUCTIONS

- ➢ Pour the pomegranate and orange juices into a pitcher with the ginger and lime slices. Overnight refrigerate.
- ➢ Discard the ginger and lime just before serving. Combine juice and club soda. As desired, garnish.

137. SPARKLING GRAPEFRUIT MOCKTAIL

Prep Time: 10 Mins

Total Time: 10 Mins

Total Time: 20 Mins

Servings: 2

INGREDIENTS

- 8 ounces of grapefruit
- 8 ounces sparkling apple-cranberry juice
- ¼ cup of chopped fresh strawberries
- Ice

INSTRUCTIONS

> ➢ Slice strawberries finely, then put 2 tbsp of the fruit in each glass. Add ice to the glass, and sprinkle it with the chopped strawberries.
> ➢ Pour 8 ounces into each glass, then fill each glass with 8 ounces of sparkling juice.
> ➢ Stir briefly to combine, then serve immediately.
> ➢ Enjoy!

138. TROPICAL COOLER

Total Time: 10 Mins

Servings: 12

INGREDIENTS

- 32 ounces of chilled cranberry juice
- 1 liter of chilled ginger ale
- 1 cup of chilled tropical fruit punch
- 1 cup of chilled orange juice
- Assorted fresh fruit or edible flowers, optional

INSTRUCTIONS

> ➢ In a punch bowl, add the first 4 ingredients right before serving. Add fruit or edible flowers as a garnish, if preferred.

139. BLACKBERRY THYME MOCKTAIL

Cook Time10 Mins

Servings: 4

INGREDIENTS

- ⅓ cup of fresh blackberries
- ⅓ cup of water
- ⅓ cup of cane sugar
- 3 sprigs of thyme
- ice
- Club soda
- Extra blackberries and thyme for garnish

INSTRUCTIONS

➢ Bring ⅓ cup of fresh blackberries, ⅓ cup of water, 1 sprig of thyme, and ⅓ cup of cane sugar to a boil in a small saucepan or skillet over medium heat. Once the fresh blackberries have softened, gently mash them in the pan.

➢ Adjust the temperature to low and simmer the syrup for 10 minutes. After the mixture has thickened for some time, pour it into a glass jar and let it cool for at least 5 minutes.

➢ Pour 1 to 2 tsp of blackberry syrup into each glass (depending on desired amount of sweetness), add ice, top with club soda, and garnish with a sprig of thyme and fresh blackberries. Before serving, stir.

➢ Use the remaining syrup to refresh the two beverages for two more servings, or keep them in a jar with a lid in the refrigerator for up to 10 days.

NOTES

1. Feel free to replace the club soda with flavored sparkling water.

140. WATERMELON LIME AGUA FRESCA

Total Time: 1 Hr 15 Mins

Servings: 10

INGREDIENTS

- 8 cups of divided water
- 5 cups of peeled, cubed and seeded watermelon
- ½ cup of white sugar, or more to taste
- ⅓ cup of lime juice, or more to taste

INSTRUCTIONS

➢ In a blender, combine 1 cup of water, watermelon, and sugar; mix until smooth. Pour into a big pitcher and add the remaining 7 cups of water. Adjust the sugar or lime juice to taste. Refrigerate for 1 hour or until cool.

141. PINK RHUBARB PUNCH

Total Time: 30 Mins

Servings: 20

INGREDIENTS

- 8 cups of chopped fresh or frozen rhubarb
- 8 cups of water
- 2-½ cups of sugar
- 2 tbsp strawberry gelatin powder
- 2 cups of boiling water
- 2 cups of pineapple juice
- ¼ cup of lemon juice
- 6 cups of chilled ginger ale
- Optional: fresh pineapple wedges, sliced strawberries, and sliced lemons

INSTRUCTIONS

➢ In a Dutch oven, bring the rhubarb and water to a boil. Reduce heat to a simmer for 10 minutes, uncovered. Drain, reserving liquid (save rhubarb for another use).
➢ Dissolve sugar and gelatin powder in hot water in a large mixing bowl. Mix in the pineapple and lemon juices. Stir in the rhubarb liquid and refrigerate until cooled.
➢ Put it into a punch bowl and stir with ginger ale just before serving. Garnish with fruit if desired.

142. SWEET SUNRISE MOCKTAIL

Total Time: 5 Mins

Servings: 1

INGREDIENTS

- Ice
- 2-3 dashes of orange bitters
- 4 ounces of orange-pineapple juice
- ½ ounce grenadine syrup
- slice of grapefruit, orange, or pineapple for garnish

INSTRUCTIONS

➢ Pour ice into a highball glass.
➢ Top with orange-pineapple juice and 2-3 dashes of orange cocktail bitters.
➢ Pour in the grenadine syrup, which will sink to the bottom and rise to the top.
➢ Garnish with a grapefruit, orange, or pineapple slice.
➢ Serve right away.

143. SPARKLING GINGER CITRUSADE

Total Time: 10 Mins

Servings: 8

INGREDIENTS

Ginger Citrusade

- 1 cup of grapefruit juice
- 1 cup of orange juice
- ½ cup of blood orange juice
- 2 ounces of lime juice
- 1 ounce of lemon juice
- 1 ½ ounces of ginger juice (extracted from 5-inch piece of peeled ginger)

Other components

- Honey syrup
- Sparkling mineral water chilled as needed
- Kosher salt to taste

INSTRUCTIONS

➤ Use a juicer to juice all the fruits and ginger. Combine everything. Refrigerate until ready to serve.

➤ To make, fill a serving glass halfway with ice and add 1/2 cup of ginger citrusade. 1 tbsp of honey syrup (or more based on your sweetness preferences). ½ Top with mineral water. Add a sprinkle of salt to taste. To combine, stir everything together. Garnish with a piece of any citrus.

NOTES

1. Don't forget the pinch of salt. It's the most important part. The salt makes the citrus flavors stronger, and it really rounds out the whole drink.
2. Refrigerate the mixed juices (together with the sparkling water) in an airtight container for up to three days.

144. CITRUS & WHITE GRAPE JUICE PARTY PUNCH

Total Time: 5 Mins

Servings: 32

INGREDIENTS

- 4 cups of chilled white grape juice
- 12 ounces of thawed, frozen lemonade concentrate
- 12 ounces thawed frozen orange juice concentrate
- 2 liters of chilled lemon-lime soda
- Optional: orange slices, lemon slices, and green grapes

INSTRUCTIONS

➢ Mix grape juice, lemonade concentrate, and orange juice concentrate in a punch bowl. Add soda, then serve right away. If preferred, add fruit as a garnish.

145. CRANBERRY-APPLE SPRITZER

Prep Time: 10 Mins

Cook Time: 3 Hr

Total Time: 3 Hr 10 Mins

Servings: 12

INGREDIENTS

- 2 liters lemon-lime soda
- 6 medium peeled and chopped apples
- 1 medium sliced navel orange
- 1 cup of fresh or frozen cranberries
- 5 cinnamon sticks (3 inches)
- 2 to 4 tbsp of honey, optional
- Apple slices

INSTRUCTIONS

➢ Combine the first 5 ingredients plus, if desired, add honey in a 4- or 5-quart slow cooker. Cook on high for 3-4 hours, or until thoroughly heated. Before serving, strain if preferred. Add apple slices and more cinnamon sticks as garnish.

146. CUCUMBER LIME MOCKTAIL

Total Time: 15 Mins

Servings: 4

INGREDIENTS

- 1 large cucumber
- 3 tbsp mint leaves
- 1 cup of water
- 2 limes
- 1 cup of carbonated mineral water
- 2 tbsp maple syrup
- 2 cups of ice cubes (additional as required)
- pinch of salt

INSTRUCTIONS

➢ 1 big cucumber, peeled and diced, added to a high-speed blender
➢ Add 1 cup of water, 2 limes' juice, 3 tbsp of mint leaves (adjust to taste), 2 tbsp of maple syrup, and a sprinkle of salt to the blender. Until smooth, blend.
➢ Strain the cucumber juice into a jar using a fine strainer or cheesecloth.
➢ Add 2 cups of ice cubes and 1 cup of carbonated mineral water to the container (you can add more ice cubes if you like).
➢ Use ice cubes to serve in glasses. Slices of cucumber, a lime wedge, and more mint can be added as a garnish.

147. PINEAPPLE HIBISCUS MOCKTAIL

Prep Time: 15 Mins

Cook Time: 15 Mins

Total Time: 30 Mins

Servings: 2

INGREDIENTS

- 2" piece of fresh ginger
- ¼ cup of sugar
- 2 ¼ cups of water, divided use
- ¼ cup of dried hibiscus petals (also called Jamaica flowers)
- ½ fresh peeled and cored pineapple
- 2 fresh cilantro sprigs

INSTRUCTIONS

- ➢ Peel the ginger and cut it into very thin pieces. Smash it up with the end of a knife, and add it to a small saucepan. Add ¼ cup of water and the sugar to the top. Bring it to a boil, then reduce the heat and simmer, covered, for 10 minutes. It will be quite aromatic. Let the side cool.
- ➢ The next step is to boil the final 2 cups of water. Turn off the heat when it begins to boil, add the hibiscus petals, and cover. Give it 15 minutes to steep. Be careful—this mixture will stain anything it touches when completed, strain and allow it to cool. (You may do this ahead of time.)
- ➢ Meanwhile, juice or mix the pineapple in a blender and strain. You may also use canned pineapple juice instead.
- ➢ Take the ginger out of the syrup mixture with a strainer, and divide the syrup mixture between two tall glasses. Add plenty of ice cubes, and then top with equal amounts of pineapple juice and hibiscus tea. Finally, bruise the cilantro with the side of the knife and add it to the glass. Serve.

NOTES

1. You can make this recipe bigger to serve a lot of people. I usually do! Just triple or treble all ingredients.

148. FESTIVE CRANBERRY COLADA

Total Time: 10 Mins

Servings: 10

INGREDIENTS

- 5 cups of cranberry juice
- 2½ cups of unsweetened pineapple juice
- 2½ cups of orange juice
- 1¼ cups of cream of coconut
- Assorted fresh fruit, optional

INSTRUCTIONS

➤ Place all ingredients in a blender in batches; cover and process until smooth. Serve with ice. If desired, garnish with fresh fruit.

149. PINEAPPLE MARGARITA MOCKTAIL

Total Time: 10 Mins

Servings: 4

INGREDIENTS

- 1 1-in. ginger piece
- 4 cups of peeled and cubed pineapple
- 4 cups of water
- ¼ cup of coconut sugar

For rim
- 1 lemon cut in half
- ¼ tsp salt
- 1 tbsp coconut sugar

INSTRUCTIONS

➢ Puree the ginger, pineapple, water, and coconut sugar until smooth. If desired, pass through a fine sieve.
➢ Immediately serve over ice.
➢ To prepare the rim
➢ Mix coconut sugar and salt on a saucer.
➢ Rub the rims of each glass with the halved lemon, then dip into the salt and coconut sugar.

150. PEACH BLUEBERRY SANGRIA MOCKTAILS

Total Time: 10 Mins

Servings: 8

INGREDIENTS

- 2 cups of blueberries
- 12 cups of fresh mint, plus more mint for garnish
- 2 sliced peaches
- 3 cups of white grape juice
- 3 cups of seltzer water
- ¼ cup of Pompeian Organic Apple Cider Vinegar

INSTRUCTIONS

➢ 1/2 cup of blueberries and mint in a drinking glass. Muddle the blueberries and mint until they are broken up and aromatic. Pour the ingredients into a big pitcher.
➢ Add the remaining blueberries, peaches, grape juice, seltzer water, and Pompeian Organic Apple Cider Vinegar to the pitcher. To combine, stir everything together.
➢ To enhance the flavors, refrigerate the pitcher for at least an hour. Pour into individual drinking glasses and garnish with fresh mint when ready to serve.

151. CITRUS CIDER PUNCH

Total Time: 5 Mins

Servings: 19

INGREDIENTS

- 1 gallon of chilled apple cider
- 12 ounces of thawed, frozen lemonade concentrate
- 1 medium sliced lemon
- 4 spiced apple rings

INSTRUCTIONS

➢ Combine cider and lemonade in a large punch bowl. Add slices of lemon and apple. Serve with more lemon slices and apple rings if preferred.

152. VIRGIN BLOODY MARY MOCKTAIL

Total Time: 5 Mins

Servings: 1

INGREDIENTS

- 1 cup of tomato juice
- 1 tbsp dill pickle juice
- 2-5 dashes Tabasco
- 2 dashes of Worcestershire sauce
- 1 tbsp lime juice
- ½ tsp celery salt

INSTRUCTIONS

➢ Stir all ingredients together in a glass of your choosing.
➢ Add a great deal of ice and garnish with celery, pickles, pickled onions, olives, and lime.

153. SCARLET SIPPER

Total Time: 5 Mins

Servings: 12

INGREDIENTS

- 4 cups of chilled cranberry-apple juice
- 1 cup of chilled orange juice
- ¼ cup of chilled lemon juice
- 1 liter of chilled ginger ale
- Optional: Fresh cranberries, orange and lemon wedges

INSTRUCTIONS

➤ In a pitcher, mix the juices and ginger ale. Serve chilled. Garnish, if preferred, with cranberries, orange, and lemon wedges.

154. HONEY GRAPEFRUIT HOLIDAY MOCKTAIL

Total Time: 10 Mins

Servings: 4

INGREDIENTS

- 2 cups of pure pineapple juice
- 1 cup of freshly-squeezed grapefruit juice
- 1 freshly-squeezed blood orange
- A handful of basil or thyme sprigs
- ⅓ cup of raw honey
- For the topping, ginger beer (You can also use another fizzy drink)

Garnish
- Pomegranate arils
- Pineapple chunks, optional
- Grapefruit wedges
- Fresh basil leaves

INSTRUCTIONS

To make mocktails

- ➤ Mix the grapefruit, blood orange, pineapple, honey, and basil in a pitcher, slightly crushing the basil leaves to bring out the taste.
- ➤ Assemblage: For each drink, fill an 8-ounce glass halfway with crushed ice. Sliced grapefruit wedges, pineapple chunks (if preferred), pomegranate seeds, and fresh basil are garnished with ½ cup of the mocktail mixture (or thyme sprigs). Add ginger beer to the remaining space in the glass.
- ➤ Sip and enjoy!

155. ALCOHOL FREE CHERRY-LIME RICKEY

Prep Time: 10 Mins

Cook Time: 2 Mins

Total Time: 12 Mins

Servings: 2

INGREDIENTS

- 6 fresh cherries, pitted and roughly chopped
- 2 ounces of fresh lime juice
- 2 ounces cherry-infused simple syrup
- chilled club soda
- ice

INSTRUCTIONS

- ➤ Mix the lime juice and fresh cherries in a tall glass or cocktail shaker.
- ➤ Next, add ice to two good-sized tumbler glasses (or one very big glass, if serving one) and top with a small sieve.
- ➤ Pour the lime and cherry mixture into the glass after straining off the cherry pieces. (We tried keeping them, but they always plug up the straw and make drinking a challenge.)
- ➤ Add the simple cherry syrup immediately, then pour the club soda on top.
- ➤ Garnish with a cherry or a lime round after a little stir.
- ➤ This drink benefits from a few minutes of rest before drinking.

NOTES

1. Either fresh or frozen cherries work well for this recipe.
2. The best lime juice is fresh juice!

156. CRANBERRY CHERRY PUNCH

Total Time: 15 Mins

Servings: 3- 1

INGREDIENTS

- ⅓ cup of fresh or frozen cranberries
- 2 lemon slices, cut into 6 wedges
- 3 ounces of cherry gelatin
- 1 cup of boiling water
- 3 cups of cold water
- 6 cups of chilled cranberry juice
- ¾ cup of thawed lemonade concentrate
- 1 liter of chilled ginger ale

INSTRUCTIONS

➢ Add a few cranberries and a slice of lemon in each ice cube tray compartment. Pour water over the mixture and freeze.
➢ Dissolve gelatin in boiling water in a punch bowl or other large container. Add the lemonade concentrate, cranberry juice, and cold water by stirring. Add ginger ale right before serving. Serve with ice cubes of cranberry and lemon.

157. STONE FRUIT THYME SHRUB SODA

Prep Time: 15 Mins

Inactive Time: 1 Day

Total Time: 1 Day 15 Mins

Servings: 1

INGREDIENTS

- 1 pound stone fruit (450g), white peaches, white nectarines, and yellow plums cut into large chunks
- ¾ cup/180ml raw light-colored honey
- 10 sprigs of fresh thyme
- ¾ cup/180ml apple cider vinegar
- Crushed ice for serving
- Sparkling mineral water for serving

INSTRUCTIONS

➢ Put the fruit in a large glass bowl or mason jar. Stir in the honey and thyme leaves, then cover. Until the fruit is syrupy, place it in the refrigerator for at least 24 hours.
➢ Strain the syrup from the fruit using a fine mesh strainer, pressing down firmly to collect all of the syrup.
➢ Add vinegar and pour into a clean container or jar. If desired, let it sit in the refrigerator for 24 hours before using it. (Store any unused portion in the fridge.)
➢ In a glass, combine ice, syrup, and sparkling water. (A good ratio is 1 part syrup to 3 parts sparkling water.)

158. STRAWBERRY DAIQUIRI MOCKTAIL

Prep time: 5 Mins

Servings: 4

INGREDIENTS

- 2 cups of frozen strawberries
- ¼ cup of simple syrup
- 2 tbsp lime juice
- 2 tbsp lemon juice
- 1 cup of Sprite
- ½ cup of water
- 1 cup of ice

INSTRUCTIONS

- ➤ First, put all ingredients in a blender and process them until they are completely smooth.
- ➤ Pour into four glasses and top with a strawberry or lime wedge from the garden.
- ➤ Enjoy while frozen.

159. EASY CITRUS SLUSH

Total Time: 15 Mins

Servings: 25

INGREDIENTS

- 2½ cups of sugar
- 3 ounces of lemon gelatin
- 3 ounces of pineapple gelatin
- 4 cups of boiling water
- 12 ounces of thawed frozen pineapple juice concentrate
- 1 cup of lemon juice
- 0.23 ounces of unsweetened lemonade mix
- 10 cups of cold water
- 2 liters chilled ginger ale
- Lime slices, optional

INSTRUCTIONS

- ➤ In a large container, combine the sugar and gelatin with boiling water and dissolve. Add the cold water, drink mix, lemon juice, and concentrated pineapple juice. Divide it, if required, among more smaller containers. Cover and freeze, mixing several times.
- ➤ Remove from the freezer 1 hour before serving. Stir the mixture until slushy. Just before serving, pour 1 liter of ginger ale into a punch bowl with 9 cups of the slush mixture. Repeat with the remaining ginger ale and slush. Garnish with lime slices if desired.

160. ORANGE AND COCONUT WATER REFRESHER

Total Time: 5 Mins

Servings: 2

INGREDIENTS

- 1 cup of freshly squeezed orange juice
- 1 cup of sparkling water
- 1 cup of coconut water
- a few springs of fresh mint
- a handful of ice cubes

INSTRUCTIONS

- ➤ Mix everything together in a pitcher.
- ➤ Serve the beverage in two glasses, and enjoy!

NOTES

1. **Substitutions:** Instead of sparkling water, you may substitute club soda.

161. THE MERRY MOCKTAIL

Total Time: 10 Mins

Servings: 4

INGREDIENTS

Rosemary Simple Syrup

- 4 cups of water
- 4 cups of sugar
- .5 ounce of fresh rosemary
- optional: 4-5 whole cloves

Merry Mocktail

- 2–3 ounces of simple rosemary syrup
- 2–3 ounces of pomegranate juice
- 2–3 ounces of club soda with a squeeze of fresh lime (OR lime-flavored bubbly water)

INSTRUCTIONS

➢ Heat the water, sugar, rosemary, and cloves in a saucepan over medium-high heat. Bring to a low boil and simmer for 5 to 10 minutes, or until the sugar has completely dissolved. To remove the cloves and stray rosemary leaves, pour through a fine-mesh strainer. Place them in glass jars and keep them in the refrigerator for 2 weeks. (I often stick a sprig of rosemary in there, so it keeps getting more intense.)

➢ Pour your preferred ratios of rosemary syrup, pomegranate juice, and limey bubbly water into a glass over an ice ball. Gently stir, taste, and adjust as desired, and enjoy.

NOTES

1. If you want to be fancy, garnish with a rosemary sprig or some fresh cranberries!
2. The rosemary sprig will drop its leaves into the simple syrup; I usually just let them sink to the bottom and pour slowly to avoid getting rosemary leaves in my drink.

162. SPARKLING COCONUT GRAPE JUICE

Total Time: 5 Mins

Servings: 6

INGREDIENTS

- 4 cups of white grape juice
- 2 tsp of lime juice
- Ice cubes
- 2 cups of chilled coconut-flavored sparkling water
- Optional: Lime wedges or slices

INSTRUCTIONS

➢ Combine grape juice and lime juice in a pitcher. Add ice to 6 large glasses. Pour the juice mixture into the glasses equally, and then top with sparkling water. To combine, stir. If desired, garnish with lime wedges.

163. PINEAPPLE PEACH AGUA FRESCA

Total Time: 30 Mins

Servings: 4

INGREDIENTS

- 3 peeled and cubed ripe peaches
- 1 cup of fresh pineapple chunks
- 2 cups of water
- 3 limes, juiced
- 2 tbsp of simple syrup
- 1 cup of frozen peach slices
- Fresh mint
- lime slices for serving

INSTRUCTIONS

- ➢ In a saucepan over medium heat, mix equal parts sugar and water (such as ¼ cup of each) to make the simple syrup. Whisk until the sugar melts, then remove from the heat and set aside to cool thoroughly.
- ➢ Blend the peaches, pineapple, and 1 cup of water in a blender until smooth. Pour the purée through a fine-mesh sieve into a big bowl or measuring cup, pressing out the last of the liquid with a spoon. Mix the juice with the remaining water, lime juice, and simple syrup in a big pitcher. If needed, taste and add extra syrup. Cool down completely. Before serving, add frozen peach slices (to serve as ice cubes!) and a few ice cubes if you want it to be really cold.
- ➢ Serve the extra lime slices and mint over ice.

164. LEMON SLUSHIES

Prep Time: 10 Mins

Cook Time: 30 Mins

Total Time: 40 Mins

Servings: 2

INGREDIENTS

- ½ cup of water
- ½ cup of granulated sugar
- 1 cup of freshly squeezed lemon juice
- 5 cups of ice
- 2 sprigs of fresh mint (optional)

INSTRUCTIONS

- ➢ In a mini saucepan over medium heat, combine ½ cup of water and ½ cup of granulated sugar; stir to combine. Remove from the heat and allow it cool for at least 30 minutes until room temperature. Meanwhile, juice 8 to 10 medium-sized lemons until you have 1 cup of juice.
- ➢ Mix 5 cups of ice in a blender with the syrup and lemon juice. Begin blending on low and gradually increase the speed until the mixture is thoroughly mixed and creamy. If desired, pour into two glasses, garnish with a mint sprig, and serve immediately.

165. PINK PARTY PUNCH

Total Time: 10 Mins

Servings: 32

INGREDIENTS

- 46 ounces of chilled white grape juice
- 48 ounces of chilled cranberry juice
- 12 ounces of thawed, frozen lemonade concentrate
- 1 liter of chilled club soda
- 2 cups of lemon sherbet or sorbet

INSTRUCTIONS

➢ Mix juices and lemonade concentrate in a large punch bowl. Stir in the club soda and top with sherbet.

166. SPARKLING BLACKCURRANT RASPBERRY MOCKTAIL

Total Time: 5 Mins

Servings: 1

INGREDIENTS

- 4 fresh raspberries
- 6-ounce Sparkling Gourmet Blackcurrant Lime sparkling water chilled
- juice from half a lime or citrus of your choice
- fresh mint to garnish

INSTRUCTIONS

➢ Use Power Sparkling to make 1 liter of cold water. Blackcurrant Lime Sparkling Gourmet Flavor.
➢ In a serving glass, muddle fresh raspberries. Place ice in the glass with the lime juice. Add chilled blackcurrant lime sparkling water. To combine, stir. Lime slices and fresh mint are used as garnish.

67. AGUA DE JAMAICA

Prep Time: 2 Mins

Cook Time: 20 Mins

Total Time: 22 Mins

Servings: 2

INGREDIENTS

- 2 quarts of water
- 1.5 cups of dried hibiscus flowers
- ⅔ cup of sugar (add more or less to taste)
- ⅓ cup of fresh orange, lemon, or lime juice (optional)

INSTRUCTIONS

- ➢ In a saucepan, bring the water to a boil. Add the sugar, and stir until dissolved. Remove from the heat, then mix in the hibiscus flours. Allow it steep for about 20 minutes, then strain out the hibiscus flowers. Stir in citrus juice if desired, then refrigerate. Serve chilled.
- ➢ You can also make this as sun tea, and let the water and hibiscus sit out in the sunlight all day.
- ➢ Also, it may go without saying, but be careful not to get the drink on your clothes when making or straining it. Those pink hibiscus leaves can stain clothes very easily!

168. WARM CHRISTMAS PUNCH

Prep Time: 5 Mins

Cook Time: 2 Hrs

Total Time: 2 Hrs 5 Mins

Servings: 8

INGREDIENTS

- 32 ounces of cranberry juice
- 6 ounces of unsweetened pineapple juice
- ⅓ cup of Red Hots
- 1 cinnamon stick (3-½ inches)
- Optional: sugared cranberries or additional cinnamon sticks

INSTRUCTIONS

➢ Combine the juices, Red Hots, and a cinnamon stick in a 3-qt slow cooker. Cover and cook on low for 2 to 4 hours, or until cooked through and candies are dissolved.
➢ Remove the cinnamon stick before serving. If preferred, garnish with sugared cranberries and more cinnamon sticks.

169. CITRUS HONEY LIME MINT MOCKTAIL

Prep Time: 5 Mins

Cook Time: 6 Mins

Steep Time: 15 Mins

Total Time: 26 Mins

Servings: 2

INGREDIENTS

Simple Honey Mint Syrup

- 2-3 cups of fresh water
- A handful of mint leaves
- ½ cup of honey

Mocktail

- 1 cup of juice of an orange
- ½ cup of lime juice
- sliced limes
- Mint leaves

INSTRUCTIONS

- ➢ To begin, add water to a medium pot and bring it to a boil over medium-high heat. Add the mint leaves and continue cooking for another 5–6 minutes.
- ➢ To ensure that the mint flavor is properly infused and potent, let the mixture steep for about 10-15 minutes after removing the mixture from the heat and gently stirring in the honey.
- ➢ Once fully steeped, discard mint leaves, pour the mixture into a medium pitcher, and place it aside.
- ➢ To Make Mocktails: pour crushed ice into a glass, ½ of the glass with Honey-Mint Syrup, ¼ of the glass with orange juice, then 2-3 tbsp of lime juice, and garnish with lime slices and mint leaves. Repeat for each serving.
- ➢ Drink and enjoy!

170. GRAPEFRUIT LIME SPRITZER

Total Time: 10 Mins

Servings: 1

INGREDIENTS

- 4 ounces of grapefruit Italian soda
- 1 ounce of freshly squeezed lime juice
- 2 to 4 ounces of club soda citrus ones are great here!
- a bunch of crushed iced
- salt + sugar for the rim

INSTRUCTIONS

➤ On a plate, combine some sugar and salt. A lime slice and salted sugar are used to rim your drink. Add ice to a glass. Stir in the lime juice and grapefruit soda. Add a few lime wedges and the club soda to top it off!

171. ICED HONEYDEW MINT TEA

Total Time: 20 Mins

Servings: 10

INGREDIENTS

- 4 cups of water
- 24 fresh mint leaves
- 8 green tea bags
- ⅔ cup of sugar
- 5 cups of diced honeydew melon
- 3 cups of ice cubes
- Additional ice cubes

INSTRUCTIONS

➤ To begin, boil the water in a large pot, then remove it from the heat. Add the tea bags and mint leaves; let the mixture steep, covered, for 3 to 5 minutes, stirring occasionally. Remove the tea and mint bags. Add sugar and mix.

➤ In a blender, combine 2-½ cups of honeydew, 2 cups of tea, and 1-½ cups of ice. Cover and mix until smooth. Serve over additional ice. Repeat with the remaining ingredients.

172. CUCUMBER GINGER MINT AGUA FRESCA

Total Time: 5 Mins

Servings: 6

INGREDIENTS

- 2 large English cucumbers, cut into chunks
- 1 cup of freshly squeezed lime juice
- ⅔ cup of granulated sugar
- 10-15 fresh mint leaves
- 1 piece of fresh ginger (1-2 inches)
- 4 cups of divided water

INSTRUCTIONS

➤ In a blender jar, combine all the prepared ingredients. Add 2 cups of water. Cover and blend until completely smooth.

➤ Over a pitcher, place a sieve. To remove the pulp, strain the agua fresca. Add the remaining 2 cups of water. Cover and chill until ready to serve.

173. FROTHY FESTIVE PUNCH

Total Time: 10 Mins

Servings: 2

INGREDIENTS

- 1½ quarts of softened vanilla ice cream
- 4 cups of cold whole milk
- 3 cups of chilled pineapple juice
- ½ cup of chilled orange juice
- 1 tbsp lemon juice
- 1 tsp vanilla extract
- ¼ tsp almond extract

INSTRUCTIONS

➤ Beat all ingredients together until frothy. Pour into a cold punch bowl. Let's stand for 15 to 20 minutes until froth comes to the top.

174. BLUEBERRY GINGER LIME NEW YEAR'S MOCKTAILS

Total Time: 5 Mins

Servings: 4

INGREDIENTS

Mocktails

- 3 cups of filtered water
- 1 cup of fresh blueberries
- ½ cup of fresh blackberries, optional
- ¼ cup of freshly squeezed lime juice
- ¼ cup of agave or Honey
- Ginger beer, for topping

Garnish

- Fresh blueberries
- Fresh blackberries
- Lime wedges
- Fresh rosemary sprigs

INSTRUCTIONS

- ➤ Combine the fresh blueberries, blackberries, and lime juice to a bowl, and mash (crush) everything together until the fruit is completely broken down. Add water and agave nectar, and stir until mixed. Depending on the desired sweetness, add more sweetener.
- ➤ **To Make Mocktails:** Add crushed ice to glass(es) or flutes. Pour ½ cup of the mocktail liquid mixture into the glass, top with ginger beer until the glass is full, and add 3-4 tbsp of mulled blackberries or blueberries. Fresh blackberries or blueberries, lime slices, and rosemary sprigs can be added as additional garnish. Repeat this for every serving.
- ➤ Enjoy Your Drink!

175. LAVENDER KUMQUAT SHRUB

Total Time: 20 Mins

Servings: 20

INGREDIENTS

For the shrub

- 1 pound of quartered whole kumquats
- 1 cup of mild honey
- 3 tbsp of lavender buds
- ½ cup of fresh lemon juice
- 1 cup of apple cider vinegar

For serving

- ice and fizzy water

INSTRUCTIONS

Make the shrub

- ➢ Mix the kumquats, honey, and lavender in a large glass bowl or jar to release the citrus juices and oils. Add the vinegar and lemon juice and stir. For two full days, cover the plant and let it at room temperature. After two days, strain the shrub, pressing on the solids to get as much liquid as possible
- ➢ For up to a month, keep the shrub in the refrigerator. Pour a few tsp into a glass to serve. 1 part shrub to 3 or 4 parts fizzy water is often about right; add ice and fizzy water till you enjoy the flavor.

176. LEMONY PINEAPPLE ICED TEA

Total Time: 20 Mins

Servings: 20

INGREDIENTS

- 16 cups of water
- 24 tea bags
- 6 fresh mint sprigs
- 3-⅓ cups of sugar
- 3 cups of unsweetened pineapple juice
- 1 cup of lemon juice

INSTRUCTIONS

- ➢ Bring water in a stockpot to a boil; remove from heat. Add the tea bags and steep for 10 minutes, covered. Discard tea bags. Steep the mint for 5 minutes. Remove the mint. Add the remaining ingredients while stirring the sugar to dissolve.
- ➢ Transfer to a covered, big container or pitcher. Refrigerate until chilled, covered. Serve with ice if preferred.

177. MOMOSAS

Total Time: 5 Mins

Servings:12

INGREDIENTS

- ½ gallon of orange juice
- ½ gallon orange sherbet
- 1 liter of sparkling mineral water with orange essence, not sweetened

INSTRUCTIONS

➤ To make individual drinks, fill champagne glasses with sherbet approximately halfway. Cover the sherbet with orange juice, then top with sparkling water. Serve it with a straw for stirring.

➤ To prepare a punch, add sherbet to a big punch bowl and split it up with a spoon. Add orange juice, then carefully pour sparkling water into the container. As you serve, often stir with a serving ladle.

178. BLACKBERRY LEMON MOCKTAIL

Prep Time: 2 Mins

Cook Time: 10 Mins

Total Time: 12 Mins

Servings: 4

INGREDIENTS

- ½ cup of fresh blackberries
- ¼ cup of sugar
- 1 cup of water
- ½ cup of pre-made lemonade
- juice of 1 lemon
- lemon slices
- seltzer/club soda
- mint

INSTRUCTIONS

- In a mini saucepan, mash the blackberries with a fork or potato masher until they are broken down into small bits.
- Put in the sugar, water, and lemonade, and bring to a simmer.
- Simmer for around 10 minutes over low to medium heat.
- Remove the blackberry bits from the mixture using a strainer, then stir in the lemon juice and chill the mixture in the refrigerator until it has chilled.
- Pour the liquid evenly among 4 glasses with ice after it has cooled.
- Fill the glass with seltzer.
- Lemon slices, mint, and extra blackberries are used as garnish.

179. ROSEMARY LEMONADE

Prep Time:10 Mins

Cook Time: 15 Mins

Total Time: 25 Mins

Servings: 8

INGREDIENTS

- 2 cups of water
- 2 fresh rosemary sprigs
- ½ cup of sugar
- ½ cup of honey
- 1-¼ cups of fresh lemon juice
- Ice cubes
- 6 cups of cold water
- Optional, extra lemon slices and rosemary sprigs.

INSTRUCTIONS

- ➢ Bring to a boil two cups of water in a small saucepan and add rosemary sprigs. Reduce heat; simmer with lid on for 10 minutes.
- ➢ Remove the rosemary and discard it. Stir in the sugar and honey until dissolved. Transfer to a pitcher and chill for 15 minutes.
- ➢ Stir in the lemon juice and cool water. Serve chilled. If desired, add more lemon slices and rosemary sprigs to the top.

180. GINGER BEER MOJITO

Total Time: 1 Mins

Servings: 1

INGREDIENTS

- 10 mint leaves
- 4 ounces of ginger beer
- 2 ounces of fresh lime juice
- ice
- garnishes: fresh lime slice or slices; fresh mint sprigs

INSTRUCTIONS

➤ In a glass, muddle the mint with the lime juice. Combine a few large ice cubes, then pour in the ginger beer. If desired, add more garnishes to the drink's finish.

➤ (After the first step, I strained out the mint leaves that I'd used to muddle with the lime juice. The lime wedges were then garnished with a few more fresh mint leaves. It's just a personal choice, but you may keep the original mint leaves in the drink if you want.)

181. PRICKLY PEAR MARGARITA MOCKTAIL RECIPE

Total Time: 5 Mins

Servings: 2

INGREDIENTS

- 1 cup of limeade
- 2 TBL fresh lime juice
- ¼ cup of simple syrup
- 2 TBL prickly pear syrup
- Club soda
- lime wedges
- sugar and salt for rim
- ice

INSTRUCTIONS

- ➤ Slice a lime and run a slice of lime around the edge of glasses.
- ➤ Put the sugar and salt mixture on the rim of your glass and set it aside.
- ➤ Mix together limeade, simple syrup, lime juice, and prickly pear syrup
- ➤ Put ice in glasses.
- ➤ In both glasses, evenly pour the mixture.
- ➤ Add club soda on top
- ➤ Garnish with a lime wedge.
- ➤ Squeeze lime into drink and enjoy!

NOTES

1. Add extra prickly pear syrup or more lime juice to adjust the sweetness if you feel it needs it.

182. CUCUMBER AGUA FRESCA

Total Time: 10 Mins

Servings: 6

INGREDIENTS

- 2 pounds of cucumber
- 2 cups of filtered water
- 3 tbsp fresh squeezed lemon juice
- 1 tbsp fresh squeezed lime juice
- ½ cup of simple syrup, or more to taste
- Simple Syrup
- 1 cup of water
- 1 cup of granulated sugar

INSTRUCTIONS

- ➤ Blend cucumber, filtered water, lime juice, and lemon juice together in a blender. Until smooth, the process.
- ➤ Using a fine strainer, strain the mixture (or a strainer lined with cheesecloth) to remove the pulp. As much liquid as you can, squeeze out. You will end up with about 4 cups of liquid. Remove pulp.

- ➤ Straining is optional but strongly recommended.
- ➤ Pour everything into a big pitcher. Add ½ cup of simple syrup for sweetness, or taste and adjust. Serve over ice and enjoy right away. Or, in an airtight jar, keep it in the refrigerator until you're ready to serve.

Simple Syrup

- ➤ In a heavy-bottom sauce saucepan, combine water and sugar. Bring to a boil on a high heat setting. Cook until the sugar has dissolved.
- ➤ Remove from heat and let cool to room temperature. Transfer to an airtight container. Up to a month in the refrigerator.

NOTES

1. Agua fresca will last up to 72 hours in the refrigerator. For best results, you should ideally eat the fresh juice within 48 hours.
2. Any cucumber variety will do (slicing or pickling). You can keep the skin on, peel some of the skin, or peel all of the skin. Keep in mind that the cucumber's skin has flavor.
3. Use fresh, firm-to-the-touch cucumbers that are fresh. Do not sure soft or soggy cucumbers.

183. STRAWBERRY WATERMELON SLUSH

Total Time: 10 Mins

Servings: 4

INGREDIENTS

- ⅓ cup of lemon juice
- ⅓ cup of sugar
- 2 cups of cubed seedless watermelon
- 2 cups of halved fresh strawberries
- 2 cups of ice cubes

INSTRUCTIONS

- ➤ Blend the first four ingredients until smooth in a blender. Add the ice and process until slushy while covered. Serve right away.

184. HUCKLEBERRY FIG SHRUB

Total Time: 15 Mins

Servings: 8

INGREDIENTS

- 1 cup of chopped fresh figs
- ½ cup of fresh or frozen huckleberries
- ¾ cup of organic blonde cane sugar
- 6 tbsp of apple cider vinegar (preferably unpasteurized)
- 6 tbsp red wine vinegar
- ice, fizzy water, and lime wedges for serving

INSTRUCTIONS

➢ Combine the figs, huckleberries, and sugar in a large glass jar or bowl. Gently mash, tightly cover, and let stand for 24 hours, frequently stirring to dissolve the sugar. After 24 hours, pass the mixture through a fine-mesh sieve to extract the liquid syrup by pressing on the solids. (The solids are good stirred into plain yogurt or mixed with more fresh fruit and baked into a crisp.) Stir the vinegar into the syrup, then pour it into a jar and place it in the refrigerator. The shrub will store for at least a month and probably longer. Pour a tbsp or two of syrup, a lime slice, and fizzy water into a glass. Stir to combine.

NOTES

1. If you cannot find huckleberries, use blackberries or wild blueberries.
2. I prefer the clean sugar flavor in this recipe, but feel free to use ½ cup of honey or ⅔ cup of grade A maple syrup.

185. PASSION FRUIT JUICE

Total Time: 10 Mins

Servings: 4

INGREDIENTS

- 1 ½ cups of filtered water
- ¾ cup of passion fruit puree
- ¼ cup of simple syrup

Simple Syrup:
- ½ cup of water
- ½ cup of granulated sugar

INSTRUCTIONS

- ➢ Fill a pitcher with filtered water, pureed passion fruit, and sweetener. To combine, stir.
- ➢ Over ice, serve chilled. Add passion fruit seeds as a garnish. Enjoy right now.
- ➢ to taste, adjust sweetness.
- ➢ Simple Syrup: Fill a small saucepot with water and sugar. Set the heat to medium. Cook the sugar until it dissolves.
- ➢ Remove from heat. Let it cool to room temperature. Pour into a container or jar. For up to two weeks, keep it covered in the refrigerator.

NOTES

1. Passion Fruit Juice = fruit puree, water, and sweetener combined.
2. Passion Fruit Puree = liquid that remains after seeds have been strained out.
3. Passion Fruit Pulp = all the bits (liquids, seeds, and all) you can scoop out within the cut passion fruit.

186. PEACH-BASIL COOLER

Total Time: 25 Mins

Servings: 12

INGREDIENTS

- 4 cups of chopped peeled fresh peaches
- 2 cups of sugar
- 1 package of fresh basil leaves
- 2 cups of cold water
- 1½ cups of fresh lemon juice
- Additional cold water
- Ice cubes
- Club soda
- Additional fresh basil leaves

INSTRUCTIONS

➤ Bring the sugar, peaches, basil, and water to a boil in a big saucepan. Reduce heat; let simmer for 5 minutes, covered. Remove from heat and leave to stand for 30 minutes. Remove the basil, then add the lemon juice. Refrigerate until thoroughly chilled.

➤ Put the peach mixture in the blender, cover it, and blend until smooth. Strain into a pitcher and adjust the consistency with extra cold water. Fill glasses with ice to serve. Pour peach mixture halfway up the glass; top with club soda. Serving with more basil.

187. CRANBERRY ORANGE KOMBUCHA

Total Time: 10 Mins

Servings: 4

INGREDIENTS

- 32 ounces of berry or cherry kombucha
- 1 large sliced orange
- 1 cup of fresh OR defrosted frozen cranberries
- Cinnamon sugar for the rims (optional)

INSTRUCTIONS

- ➤ Put the sliced oranges and cranberries in a pitcher. Stir in the kombucha until well combined.
- ➤ Wet the glass rims and then roll them in the cinnamon sugar.
- ➤ Fill each glass with ice, then add kombucha and a little of the fruit. Serve.

188. TROPICAL JACKFRUIT SMOOTHIE

Total Time: 5 Mins

Servings: 1

INGREDIENTS

- 7 pieces of fresh jackfruit
- ¼ cup of frozen banana slices
- ½ cup of frozen mango chunks
- ½ cup of well-shaken canned coconut milk, unsweetened
- ⅓ cup of pineapple juice

INSTRUCTIONS

- ➤ Place all the ingredients in a blender. Process until smooth. Serve immediately.

NOTES

1. Fresh banana and mango can be substituted for frozen. However, the resulting smoothie will not be as thick.
2. This is made creamy and rich with coconut milk. You may also use coconut water as a substitute for a lighter beverage.

189. WATERMELON-LIME COOLER

Total Time: 10 Mins

Servings: 12

INGREDIENTS

- 12 cups of divided cubed seedless watermelon, frozen
- ¾ tsp divided grated lime zest
- 6 cups of divided chilled ginger ale

INSTRUCTIONS

➢ In a blender, combine 2 cups of ginger ale, ¼ tsp lime zest, and 4 cups of frozen watermelon. Cover and mix until slushy. Serve right away. Do it twice.

190. RHUBARB SHRUB RECIPE

Total Time: 15 Mins

Servings: 12

INGREDIENTS

- 2 cups of fruit – rhubarb, diced into tiny ¼-inch pieces (or use other fruit or berries)
- 1 cup of vinegar (white or apple cider, or any other)
- 1 cup of sugar

INSTRUCTIONS

➢ In a small bowl, mix the rhubarb and granulated sugar. Cover with plastic wrap and refrigerate for 4-5 days, stirring every 12 hours. Press down hard on the solids and strain the liquid. In a container with a cover, combine the rhubarb syrup and vinegar. Store it in the fridge. You may use them immediately, but their flavors will deepen, meld, and harmonize after a week. Add to sparkling water or drinks.

➢ This will keep up to a year.

191. MANDARIN LIME SPRITZ

Total Time: 5 Mins

Servings: 4

INGREDIENTS

- 2 cups of freshly squeezed mandarin juice
- ¼ cup of freshly squeezed lime juice
- handful of fresh mint leaves
- 1 ½ cups of sparkling water or club soda
- ice and mandarin segments for serving

INSTRUCTIONS

➢ Gently crush or tear the mint leaves and put them in the bottom of each glass. Pour the lime juice and mandarin juice into the glass and mix to blend. Mix in a handful of ice and some mandarin segments. Fill the glass with sparkling water and gently stir. Garnish with mint and serve right away.

192. RAINBOW SPRITZER

Total Time: 20 Mins

Servings: 4

INGREDIENTS

- ½ cup of fresh blueberries
- ½ cup of chopped peeled kiwifruit
- ½ cup of chopped fresh pineapple
- ½ cup of sliced fresh strawberries or fresh raspberries
- 1 cup of chilled ginger ale
- ½ cup of chilled unsweetened pineapple juice
- ½ cup of chilled lemonade

INSTRUCTIONS

➤ Layer blueberries, kiwis, pineapple, and strawberries in 4 tall glasses. Combine remaining ingredients in a 2-cup glass measure or small pitcher; pour over fruit. Serve right away.

193. ALCOHOL-FREE PINEAPPLE-MINT MARGARITAS

Total Time: 10 Mins

Servings: 4

INGREDIENTS

- 1 ½ cups of frozen pineapple in chunks
- ¼ cup of mint leaves
- 1 jalapeño
- 2 tbsp of agave syrup
- 3 tbsp of lemon juice
- ½-1 cup of water

INSTRUCTIONS

➢ In a blender, combine all the ingredients.
➢ Serve in glasses with a salted rim and ice.

NOTES

1. to make the margarita glass's salted rim. Pass a lemon around the rim of the glass, then place it on a plate with salt.

194. STRAWBERRY GINGER LIMEADE

Total Time: 10 Mins

Servings: 8

INGREDIENTS

- 2 ½ cups of water
- 1 cup of granulated sugar
- 1 cup of freshly squeezed lime juice
- 22 ounces of sliced strawberries, hulled
- 3-inch piece peeled and split into disks ginger

INSTRUCTIONS

➢ Bring 1 cup of water and 1 cup of sugar to a boil in a small saucepan. Cook until the sugar has dissolved. Remove from heat and allow to cool.
➢ Mix the simple cooled syrup, lime juice, cut strawberries, and ginger in a blender until smooth. Through a fine strainer, pour (or cheesecloth).
➢ Pour limeade into a pitcher. Add the remaining 1 1/2 cups of water and stir. If required, taste and add additional water. Cover and chill in the refrigerator until serving.
➢ Serve with ice, strawberry slices, and lime wedges.

195. BLACKBERRY LEMONADE

Total Time: 20 Mins

Servings: 2

INGREDIENTS

- 4 cups of divided water
- 1 cup of sugar
- 1 cup of lemon juice
- 1 tbsp grated lemon zest
- 1 cup of blackberries
- 1–2 drops of blue food coloring, optional

INSTRUCTIONS

- ➢ In a big saucepan, bring 2 cups of water and sugar to a boil. Boil for 2 minutes, stirring occasionally. Turn off the heat. Add the lemon juice, zest, and remaining water; stir. Let it cool slightly.
- ➢ In a blender, combine 1 cup of the lemon mixture with the blackberries; blend until smooth: strain and discard seeds. Pour the remaining lemon and blackberry mixture into a pitcher and stir well. If desired, add food coloring. Place it in the refrigerator until cooled. Serve with ice in cold glasses.

196. HONEY, BLACKBERRY AND SAGE REFRESHER

Total Time: 10 Mins

Servings: 2

INGREDIENTS

- 8 fresh blackberries plus more for garnish
- 10 sage leaves plus additional leaves for garnish
- ¼ cup of honey
- 2 tbsp of fresh lime juice
- 2 cups of divided seltzer water
- ½ cup of ginger beer or ginger ale

INSTRUCTIONS

- ➤ Mix the blackberries, honey, and sage well in a cocktail shaker. If needed, use ice to help mash the ingredients together.
- ➤ To mix the lime juice and ginger beer, cover the container and shake.
- ➤ Put ice in two glasses and strain the mixture into them.
- ➤ Add 1 cup of seltzer to the top of each glass.
- ➤ then serve with sage leaves and blackberries as garnish.

197. MIXED BERRY PUNCH

Total Time: 10 Mins

Servings: 2

INGREDIENTS

- 1 envelope unsweetened mixed berry mix
- 2 quarts of water
- ¾ cup of sugar
- 46 ounces chilled pineapple juice
- 1-liter chilled ginger ale

INSTRUCTIONS

- ➤ Combine the drink mix, water, and sugar in a large pitcher; stir until the sugar is dissolved; then refrigerate. Pour into a punch bowl just before serving; add pineapple juice and ginger ale.

198. CALAMANSI JUICE

Total Time: 10 Mins

Servings: 6

INGREDIENTS

- 1 cup of freshly squeezed calamansi juice, discard seeds and skin
- ¾ -1 cup of simple syrup, depending on sweetness desired
- ice, to serve
- 2 cups of water

Simple Syrup:

- 1 cup of water
- 1 cup of granulated sugar

INSTRUCTIONS

- ➢ Combine calamansi juice, water, and ¾ cup of simple syrup in a pitcher. To combine, stir. Place in refrigerator to cool.
- ➢ Stir before serving. Serve with ice. To your taste, add extra water or simple syrup.
- ➢ Simple Syrup:
- ➢ Take from heat and let cool to room temperature. Store excess syrup in the fridge and use within 2 weeks.

199. SPARKLING PEACH BELLINIS

Total Time: 35 Mins

Servings: 12

INGREDIENTS

- 3 medium peaches, halved
- 1 tbsp honey
- 11.3 ounces of chilled peach nectar
- 750ml of sparkling grape juice

INSTRUCTIONS

- ➤ Preheat the oven to 375 degrees. Line a large baking sheet with heavy-duty foil (about 18x12 in.). Place the peach halves on the foil, cut sides up, and drizzle with honey. Fold the foil over the peaches and seal them.
- ➤ Bake until soft, about 25 to 30 minutes. Cool completely; remove and discard peels. Process peaches in a food processor until smooth.
- ➤ Place the peach puree in a pitcher. Stir in the nectar and sparkling grape juice until well combined. Pour the remaining sparkling grape juice into 12 wine glasses. Serve right away.

200. ICED MELON MOROCCAN MINT TEA

Total Time: 20 Mins

Servings: 5

INGREDIENTS

- 2 cups of water
- 12 fresh mint leaves
- 4 individual green tea bags
- ⅓ cup of sugar
- 2-½ cups of diced honeydew melon
- 1-½ cups of ice cubes
- Additional ice cubes

INSTRUCTIONS

- ➤ Bring to a boil the water in a large saucepan. Remove it from the heat and stir in the mint and tea bags. Steep for 3-5 minutes, covered. Remove the mint and tea bags. Stir the sugar in.
- ➤ Blend honeydew in a blender until smooth. 1 ½ cups of ice and tea; process until smooth. Serve with more ice.

201. SPARKLING BLUEBERRY LEMONADE

Total Time: 5 Mins

Servings: 1

INGREDIENTS

- ½ cup of fresh blueberries
- 2 tsp of agave syrup or more according to taste
- ⅓ cup of freshly squeezed lemon juice
- ¾ cup of sparkling water

INSTRUCTIONS

- ➤ Combine blueberries and agave syrup in a serving glass and stir. Pour in the lemon juice. Add ice to the glass. Add sparkling water. Stir to blend.

202. RHUBARB MINT TEA

Prep Time: 15 Mins

Cook Time: 45 Mins

Total Time: 1 Hr

Servings: 12

INGREDIENTS

- 4 cups of chopped fresh or frozen rhubarb
- 2 cups of fresh or frozen raspberries
- ¾ ounce of each fresh mint leaves
- 3 quarts of water
- 4 black tea bags
- 2 cups of sugar
- 12 mint sprigs

INSTRUCTIONS

➤ Bring rhubarb, raspberries, mint, and water to a boil in a 6-quart stockpot. Simmer for 30 minutes, uncovered, on low heat. Remove from heat. Add the tea bags; steep them under cover for 3-5 minutes, as needed. Use a strainer with a fine mesh, filter the tea, removing the tea bags and pulp. Add the sugar and mix until it is dissolved. Let it cool. Transfer to a pitcher, and refrigerate until thoroughly chilled. Serve with mint sprigs on top of the ice.

203. MANGO MINT LIMEADE SLUSH

Total Time: 5 Mins

Servings: 4

INGREDIENTS

- 4 cups of frozen mango chunks
- ⅓ cup of fresh squeezed lime juice
- 2 cups of coconut water
- 8 fresh mint leaves
- 3 Tbsp simple syrup

INSTRUCTIONS

➢ Blend frozen mango chunks with lime juice, coconut water, mint leaves, and simple syrup in a blender. Mix until smooth.

➢ Depending on the sweetness of the mango, adjust the quantity of simple syrup to taste. Add lime wedges, mango chunks, or fresh mint leaves as a garnish. Serve right away.

NOTES

1. Simple Syrup: Bring ½ cup of water and ½ cup of granulated sugar to a boil. Take from heat and let cool to room temperature. For up to a month, keep it in the refrigerator in an airtight container.

204. BLUEBERRY LIME SLUSH

Total Time: 5 Mins

Servings: 20

INGREDIENTS

- 2 cups of sugar
- 4 cups of water
- 12 ounces of frozen limeade concentrate
- 12 ounces of frozen orange juice concentrate
- 2 cups of blueberry juice
- 2 liters of regular or diet lemon-lime soda, chilled
- Fresh or frozen blueberries, optional

INSTRUCTIONS

➢ In a large saucepan, add the sugar and water; bring to a boil, stirring to dissolve the sugar. 30 minutes to cool.

➢ Combine juice concentrates and blueberry juice in syrup; divide mixture (approximately 2 cups of each) among five 1-½-pint freezer containers. Freeze overnight or until firm, covered.

➢ Pour one portion of the frozen mixture and 1-⅔ cups of soda into a blender for each four-serving batch. Cover and mix until smooth. Serve right away. Serve with blueberries if preferred.

205. COLD BREW HIBISCUS TEA

Time: 12 Hr 5 Mins

Servings: 4

INGREDIENTS

Hibiscus tea

- ½ cup of dried hibiscus
- 4 cups of cool water
- optional: cinnamon stick or handful of fresh mint leaves

Simple Syrup

- 1 cup of water
- 1 cup of granulated sugar
- optional flavor: cinnamon stick or handful of torn mint leaves

INSTRUCTIONS

Hibiscus Tea

- ➤ Combine the dried hibiscus and any spices or herbs in a large pitcher. Add 4 cups of water. Place the container in the refrigerator for up to 24 hours with the lid on.
- ➤ Remove dried hibiscus from tea and discard.
- ➤ Use simple syrup to sweeten tea as desired. Start with ⅓ cup of simple syrup for a lightly sweetened tea or up to 1 cup for a sweet drink. Refrigerate until ready to serve. Serve over plenty of ice.

Simple Syrup

- ➤ In a saucepan, mix the sugar and water. Bring to a boil over medium heat until the sugar is dissolved. Remove from heat and place in another container. Once at room temperature, keep in the refrigerator.
- ➤ To produce simple flavored syrup, combine spices or herbs with water and sugar in a sauce pot. When the sugar dissolves, boil it. Put a lid on after removing it from the heat. Steep herbs and spices for 15 to 20 minutes. Taste; if you like a stronger taste, steep it longer. Place in an airtight container and keep chilled.

NOTES

1. Hibiscus tea can be kept in the fridge for up to a week.
2. Simple syrup may be refrigerated for 1 month.

Printed in Great Britain
by Amazon

18485019R00095